Douglas G. Glasgow

The Black Underclass

Poverty, Unemployment, and Entrapment of Ghetto Youth

 Jossey-Bass Publishers

San Francisco • Washington • London • 1980

THE BLACK UNDERCLASS
Poverty, Unemployment, and Entrapment of Ghetto Youth
by Douglas G. Glasgow

Copyright © 1980 by: Jossey–Bass Inc., Publishers
433 California Street
San Francisco, California 94104

&

Jossey–Bass Limited
28 Banner Street
London EC1Y 8QE

Library of Congress Cataloging in Publication Data

Glasgow, Douglas G
    The Black underclass.

    Bibliography: p. 197
    Includes index.
    1. Afro-American youth—Employment. 2. Afro-
Americans—Economic conditions. I. Title.
E185.86.G54   331.3'46396073   79–28310
ISBN 0–87589–392–9

Manufactured in the United States of America

JACKET DESIGN BY WILLI BAUM

FIRST EDITION

Code 8006

The Jossey-Bass
Social and
Behavioral Science Series

To Rickie and Karen

Preface

Over the past fifteen years, the nation's inner cities have witnessed the growth and consolidation of a population of poor and unused Black youth, confined in economic poverty and social decay. A significantly younger population than the poor of previous generations, these young Blacks, some as young as thirteen or fourteen, are already earmarked for failure—they are undereducated, jobless, without salable skills or the social credentials to gain access to mainstream life. They are rendered obsolete before they can even begin to pursue a meaningful role in society. Of the hundreds of thousands of destitute Black men and women who constitute this nation's underclass, young Black males represent the fastest growing portion. Their plight—along with their hopes, aspirations, and ultimate despair—is the focus of this book.

The Black Underclass is, intentionally, written from a Black perspective as a way to convey the special ethnocentric perceptions of those confined to ghetto survival. Many others have studied populations of poverty-stricken and socially "alienated" Blacks; indeed, the concept of the underclass is not new, nor is the reality of the Black ghetto. In the sixties, social scientists identified "pockets of poverty," and this phrase was to shape federal and local programs for a decade or more. If the "pockets" could be eliminated, then the "problem" could be solved. Although some analysts suggested that structural factors inherent in American society contributed to the entrapment of Blacks, no one addressed the need to change the basic, underlying patterns that excluded so many Blacks from participation in mainstream life.

It is my belief that such programs as the War on Poverty failed because they were based on analyses that were, at best, misinformed. Not only were many inaccurate assumptions made about the aspirations and capabilities of Black people, but these assumptions were used to justify the perpetuation of mainstream control. Psychosocial models of analysis posited that the condition of Blacks was due to individual deficits—Blacks did not have the capacity to do better, but more important they did not have the motivation to "succeed." That condition was further said to stem from a culture and a family system whose values and organization were in disarray.

The present work takes a different posture and examines the impact of mainstream institutional practices and market dynamics (most specifically, the employment realities of poor Blacks) on a group of inner-city males seeking mobility. The men whom I studied in Watts, mostly transplants from the rural South in the late forties and fifties, had looked to the big city as an opening to a better life. Although they wanted to surpass the social status of their parents—and which could have been expected if standard mobility theories had held true—no such mobility was possible for them. A decade or so after their move to the city, having been repeatedly rejected by mainstream institutions, they remained without skills and without jobs. By 1965, they were the core of Watt's youthful underclass.

One purpose of this book is to show what institutional rejection can do to individual aspirations. Among other things, the following chapters examine the lives of inner-city young men through their perceptions of their life experiences. There is a pattern to these experiences in relation to encounters with mainstream institutions, programs, procedures, and processes. It is this pattern I have attempted to capture, for it reveals more eloquently than sociological jargon what it is like to be poor, unskilled, jobless, and detached from mainstream society. Although the initial data of this work were gathered fifteen years ago, follow-up research in 1975 and my continuing studies of ghetto life have corroborated the central concerns expressed originally by the young men in Watts. If anything, these concerns are more intensely felt now than in 1965—time has not changed the realities of the underclass, it has intensified them.

A second goal of this book is to identify some major components of the mainstream that work to entrap Blacks into the underclass status. Indeed, the conceptual framework of this study holds that structural factors in the organization of our society are directly or indirectly responsible for the development of the underclass. Further, it holds that institutional racism first initiates and later supports the exclusion of Black youth from the normal paths of achievement and fulfillment. Theories of individual deficits or cultural disadvantage are neither sufficient nor accurate explanations. Too little attention has been paid to economic factors, especially over the past two decades, which have produced and maintained an increasing number of Black youths in poverty. A sluggish domestic market, technological streamlining of production processes, and the growing reliance on overseas labor for domestic goods—all have made inroads on the entry-level job market traditionally available for minority populations. Such market dynamics, when coupled with institutional racism, account for the disproportionate number of young Blacks shut off from mainstream opportunity and represent the major force propelling young Blacks into the underclass.

But this book seeks to do more than to illustrate the disillusioned hopes of Black youth or to identify the societal factors that perpetuate the underclass. It attempts to specify why, good intentions notwithstanding, efforts to improve life for the inner-city poor have failed. Part of the reason is that these programs have been aimed at correcting superficial inequities without addressing the ingrained societal factors that maintain such inequities. We need to examine what approaches have not worked in the past, why they have not worked, and how we can design and implement policies that can reverse underclass growth. Since the economic factors mentioned earlier will continue to operate in the eighties and beyond, the crisis of Black unemployment will also remain—and it threatens the secure balance of the entire society. This work suggests alternate ways to use current resources for an effective, broad-based attack on inner-city decay and underclass development. It addresses the special role that Blacks must play in terms of community reconstruction and development. There are no "guaranteed" solutions, but there are better ways to fight poverty and social displacement than have been tried in the past.

It is my hope that everyone concerned with the human, social, and economic waste represented by America's inner cities will benefit from reading this book. Those who work in government programs or for privately sponsored groups, especially policy makers and program developers, may reconsider the premises upon which they base their decisions and devise a new strategy to aid the Black poor. Elected officials at federal, state, and local levels may gain insights to the kinds of legislation that could change—rather than maintain—Black underclassness. Human services professionals who work, either directly or indirectly, with the entrapped Black population may better understand all the factors contributing to the underclass—and thereby work more effectively to nourish the capabilities and motivations of Blacks, especially of young, inner-city Black males.

Finally, it is my hope that this book will speak most forcefully to the community of Blacks. In whatever profession or of whatever social status, Black people are the single strongest resource available to reverse underclass growth. The ghetto hurts all Blacks, not just those entrapped in it. Talent and energy need to be reinvested in the inner cities by those who have made it into the mainstream. Individual successes cannot be ensured in a system that maintains institutional racism, that perpetuates inefficient and inequitable social and welfare programs, that contributes continually to the numbers of the Black underclass. An overall strategy needs to be developed—one that is directed at altering structural factors in society and responding to market dynamics. The thrust will need to come from many directions, but Black people could be the spearhead of that thrust by working to build an inner-city infrastructure that provides economic and social support for the ghetto-entrapped poor.

In sum, then, this book is not intended as a definitive study of the Black underclass. Rather, by concentrating on a group of representative young men and their individual (and collective) confrontations with mainstream institutions, it attempts to convey the human experience of those who are denied upward mobility and are processed into underclass status; to open up for consideration more effective ways for both the public and private sectors to aid urban development; and to suggest how Black expertise can be the much-needed spearhead in the revitalization of our inner cities.

Acknowledgments

I am especially indebted to the Sons of Watts, young men who shared their life experiences and provided the data for this work.

To Billy J. Tidwell, advisor to the Sons of Watts and a colleague who early recognized the importance that this experience be documented; who made my work possible; and, in the end, who provided critical ongoing reviews of much of the material.

To Betti Whaley and Afia Smallwood, whose acute editorial comments and endless patience helped to frame the book's perspective.

To Margaret Washnitzer and Barbara Bates, whose review of drafts and technical inputs aided in the final production.

And to Elaine Anderson, who provided the author invaluable sustaining support during the latter years of this production.

Part of this work was initially published in the author's doctoral dissertation and was supported by a grant from the National Institute of Mental Health.

Washington, D.C.　　　　　　　　DOUGLAS G. GLASGOW
January 1980

Contents

Contents

The Author

DOUGLAS G. GLASGOW is professor of social welfare and former dean of the School of Social Work at Howard University.

Born and raised in Bedford-Stuyvesant and Brooklyn, Glasgow was awarded the B.A. degree in sociopsychology from Brooklyn College (1959), the M.S.W. degree in social research from Columbia University (1961), and the D.S.W. degree in social research from the University of Southern California (1968).

He is a member of several professional associations, including the National Association of Social Workers, the Association for the Study of Afro-American Life and History, and the International Council of Social Welfare Education. He is a founder of the National Association of Black Social Workers and has supported the development of the United Black Fund/United Way of Washington, D.C. He is on the Citizens' Advisory Committee to the District of Columbia Bar Association and the National Advisory Committee to the Boys Club of America Health Services and Education Project. He serves as a consultant to the Department of Health, Education, and Welfare and to members of the Congressional Black Caucus.

Among other honors, Glasgow received a senior stipend award from the National Institute of Mental Health to study social welfare systems in nine African countries. He has written approximately thirty journal articles on a variety of topics pertaining to human services and Black community development.

The Black Underclass

Poverty, Unemployment, and Entrapment of Ghetto Youth

1

Black Perspectives
on the Underclass

This book was born in flames, in an inferno that raged for four August days in 1965. The place was Watts, Los Angeles; the young men who ignited it were typical of ghetto youth across the country. For nearly a decade they had gathered daily in the parking lot adjacent to the Jordan Downs Housing Project. Although they passed most of their waking hours together, they were different from the organized gangs of the eastern ghettos. What held them loosely together was their common condition: They were jobless and lacked salable skills and the opportunities to get them; they had been rejected and labeled as social problems by the police, the schools, the employment and welfare agencies; they were victims of the new camouflaged racism. For in addition to discrimination based on race, they were now rejected by "social profile." Detached from the broader white society, even largely from the seemingly complacent working Blacks around them, they drank, gambled, fought a little, but mostly just generally "hung out."

But suddenly something snapped. All the frustration and resentment burst out in a drama that will have a permanent place in Black history. And like a spark flying through a volatile atmosphere, the actions of these young men set off similar behavior by other poverty-bound youth in almost every major city in the following four years.

I can vividly recall sitting in front of my television set, watching the smoke and flames belching from the buildings on 103rd Street, listening to the narrator attempting to explain what was happening. People called me, asking, "Where the hell is Watts?" and "What's going on?" There was an ominous fear mixed with excitement all the way from the hills of Altadena, some sixty miles distant, through Pasadena to Los Angeles, from the Baldwin Hills to Avalon. And although I had only begun to know Watts—as I was a newcomer to the Red Rooster, the Parking Lot, and the many local stores—I sensed that this explosion was something different. For one thing, the Black-white confrontation characteristic of past race riots was absent: here, young Blacks set fire to buildings in their own community, dramatically chanting, "Burn, baby, burn!" For another, the first feelings of charged anger were soon replaced by a lightness and exhilaration, almost a party-time mood. This then settled into the quiet determination and actions of justification that motivated the second stage of Operation Burn, Baby, Burn. The young men of the community were joined by many other neighborhood residents in seizing household goods from burning stores. There was a new unity among the generations and the classes. The slogan "Burn, baby, burn!" had become not just the chant of the young but a silently repeated rhythm emanating from the hearts of large numbers of Blacks, many of whom would not themselves go out in the streets but remembered the forecast of *The Fire Next Time* (Baldwin, 1963).

Afterward, I sensed a new tone among the street youth of Watts. They had lost some of the quiet sullenness so typical of their Parking Lot attitudes and become vocal, animated, excited, involved. Like some strange alchemy, they adopted seemingly overnight something called Blackness. They disclaimed what had been fought for by the older generation; they were no longer to be Negroes, they were now Black. The transformation was expressed in new dialogue, a new prose, with a distinct rhythmic rhetoric; it took expression in Rastafarian and Afro hairdos, and later a new style of pigtails, called cornrows; and there were some intricate handshakes and palm slapping accompanied by smiles and intense greetings. Black folk throughout Los Angeles reconnected with their earlier communicative and expressive ways. Yes, Black people—men and women, young brothers and sisters—spoke to each other openly in these urban ghettos and seemingly without fear. And even middle-class Blacks, those who continued to function in mainstream, searched out other Blacks in seas of whites for some eye contact, ethnic recognition, some home-base touching. In the midst of white society's criticism of the unruly ghetto youths, Blacks as a whole felt closer to one another than they had for years.

Yet, these liberating consequences were not to last. (See Chapters Seven and Eight, where the explosion and its aftermath are treated in greater detail.) This is a case study of what can happen when young people are trapped in poverty and hopelessness and society becomes remiss in the performance of its duty. It is important first to talk in a broad and theoretical way about the nature of this trap: who is caught in it and why, what maintains it, and how this study began.

Emergence of the Underclass

The young firebrands of Watts were (and nearly all still are) part of what has recently been dubbed the *underclass*, a group whose emergence as a permanent fixture of our nation's social structure represents one of the most significant class developments in the past two decades. The term *underclass* has slowly, almost imperceptibly eased its way into the nation's vocabulary, subtly conveying the message that another problematic group is emerging that needs society's help. While still somewhat unclearly defined, and even thought by some not to be deserving of serious attention, a permanently entrapped population of poor persons, unused and unwanted, accumulated in various parts of the country. Although Myrdal early cited the existence of an underclass, little serious attention had been given to the idea that such a group would become a fixed part of the American economy, since upward social mobility was alleged to be the norm for those who participate in a free enterprise economy. For this reason, even when in the sixties the plight of the nation's poor once again surfaced, it was viewed as involving some isolated "pockets of poverty" whose populations required some programmatic interventions to move them from poverty to a stable income earning state. In fact, a war against poverty was launched with the view that in a few years the condition would be eradicated. However, as the sixties waned and the seventies developed, the war was assessed to be an abominable failure as social analysts, sociologists, and social workers pondered why had the poor not been eliminated, and why were there poor people in the seventies, and most disconcerting, why were there to be, and who were to be, the poor in the eighties?

As the seventies draw to a close, an examination of the populations that constitute the nation's poor discloses some important new relationships. Whereas the traditional groups that made up the poor were usually identified as the immigrant, or new migrant who moved from one area of the country to another seeking work, or as the aged, the disabled, and handicapped, currently the ranks of the poor are not being swelled by newcomers or the traditionally socially needy groups, but rather by the children of previously poor families. Therefore, poor families of the fifties and sixties were more likely to have offspring who were poor in the seventies. And Blacks, who have consistently represented a disproportionately high percentage of the nation's poor over the past three decades, not only continue to hold this unenviable distinction, but the children and offspring of their families constitute the poor in the seventies and are the projected poor of the eighties. Structural factors found in market dynamics and institutional practices, as well as the legacy of racism, produce and then reinforce the cycle of poverty and, in turn, work as a pressure exerting a downward pull toward underclass status.

While national statistics and government reports cite the improved economic condition of Blacks, despite some recent changes in the statistical configurations regarding economic status, the Black community remains in a state of continuing economic crisis. This fact is represented by the high proportion of persons who are jobless, unemployed, welfare dependent, and without sufficient incomes to secure a decent quality of life.

A government report (U.S. Bureau of the Census, 1979) suggests that a significant rise in the economic status of Blacks occurred from 1959 through 1974, citing an overall decrease in the level of Black unemployment and a growth in the numbers of Blacks who have achieved middle-class status. The fact is that unemployment decreased for both Black and white during this same period. However, from 1959 to 1974, white's rate of unemployment decreased by 43 percent (that is, from 28.3 million to 16.3 million), liquidating almost one half of the poverty group, while Black unemployment during this same period decreased by only 23 percent (that is, from 9.9 million to 7.5 million), liquidating less than one fourth of its poverty population. In fact the gap between Black and white unemployment widened, not narrowed, as the proportion of poor who were Blacks rose from 26 percent to 29 percent. Most of the decreased unemployment took place between 1959 and 1969. The proportion of Blacks in poverty showed little or no change between 1969 and 1974. And in both 1959 and 1974, the poverty rate for Blacks was about three times that for whites. These two last factors, namely the stabilization of a poverty population among Blacks and the permanent (and ever-widening) gap between Black and white unemployment (there has been a greater reduction in the number of low-income whites than Blacks over this period), highlight the economic crisis of the growing Black underclass.

A second misconstrued notion regarding Black economic progress is the contention that there has been a significant movement of Blacks into middle-class status in the past three decades. For example, the latest Census report notes that there has been an important "increase in the proportion of families with incomes over $10,000 as indicated by the fact that in 1947, only 8 percent of Black families had incomes of $10,000 or more compared with about 39 percent in 1974" (U.S. Bureau of the Census, 1979, p. 26). What these figures fail to show is that although there has been some increase in median incomes for some Black families, "the change in the main was due to the increased numbers of Black families with both husband and wife employed. As individual wage earners, Black males and females earn less than whites in comparable jobs, so that over the past quarter of a century the gains in income for Black men were somewhat less striking than those recorded for Black women. In addition, the gains in the income for Black women relative to white women were more pronounced than the gains realized by Black men relative to white men. . . . From 1948 to 1974, the median income of Black women rose by 178 percent, from $1,010 to $2,810, whereas the median income for Black men rose by 92 percent, from $2,790 to $5,370" (U.S. Bureau of the Census, 1979, p. 28). And although there has been an increase in the median individual income over the past quarter century, clearly these incomes remain small, and only in combination could they approximate a middle-class income. Attaining middle-class status has taken place primarily within young households (husband under thirty-five years) and comprised only a very small proportion (6 percent) of all Black families in the country in 1974.

A real problem reflecting the economic crisis facing Blacks is found in the large numbers of long-term, persistently poor, and immobile Blacks that persist from one generation to the next. Although reports note a decrease in Black unemployment during the past decade (1959–1969), improving a condition where better than one out of every two Blacks (55 percent in 1959) were poor, nevertheless, in 1969 one of every three Blacks still remained poor. Also, the proportion of Blacks remaining in poverty showed little or no change between 1969 and 1974. As indicated earlier, the ferocity of unemployment, joblessness, and abject poverty affects Black youth the greatest. For example, in the period 1967 through 1977, the Washington office of the Urban Coalition charted unemployment rates for Black youth between the ages of 16 and 19, showing an increase from 25.3 percent to 35.2 percent during this period. The National Urban League (NUL) has also pointed to the severe crisis among Black youth, noting "the most serious problems confronting Black America are its intolerably high level of unemployment, especially among young Blacks" (Williams, 1979,

p. i). In 1978, employing the NUL Hidden Unemployment Index, their survey showed that "business in general has not been responsive to the employment needs of minority youth, despite the grim statistics that show black youth unemployment at over 50 percent in 1978" (Williams, 1979). Clearly, then, joblessness and unemployment have become for so many youthful Blacks a way of life, a daily condition rather than a temporary one. The lack of opportunity to work and to gain a regular and sound income in the primary labor market results in many young Blacks being locked permanently into the underclass.

Escaping underclass entrapment is not determined simply by having a job or income. The many Black working poor who remain in poverty exemplifies the contradiction where one fulfills the work ethic, holds a job, and yet remains immobile and poor. The type of job—whether it provides for continuous full-time employment, upgrading, seniority protections, or other provisions aiding mobility—and the amount of pay have much to do with the ability to withstand the structural, induced downward pull toward underclass status which surrounds the Black poor.

Further, the underclass entrapment of poor Blacks is furthered by their lack of connections with standardized institutions that act as feeder systems to the primary labor market. That is, the lack of ties to unions, private industry, civil service or social agencies (professional, civic, or quasi-socioeconomic), or sanctioning institutions (education, banking, and crediting) results in the Black poor having to negotiate the labor market as individuals, ones who at best receive only partial information about its operations and openings. This is why so many Blacks who made it into the mainstream in the 1940s and 1950s, when asked how they did so while other colleagues and classmates did not, explain the occurrence by citing "chance." "I was lucky, just happened to be leaning on the door when it opened." This does not mean that they did not prepare, or did not have some organizational affiliations (usually Black), were not trying, but rather the factor of chance, more than systemal connections, was at work. The problem of today's even poorer, inner-city youth is somewhat different, as they are even less connected to any institutional network to help them "enter" the job market. They are, therefore, easily programmed "out," particularly in a market where the demand for unskilled entry-level manpower has significantly diminished. Inner-city youth represent the weakest applicants in the job world, since the labor market as a system holds no obligation to them as individuals.

The underclass is distinguished from the lower class principally by its lack of mobility. According to classical definitions, the lower-class experience is a variation of middle-class adaptation and striving. The perennial expressions "I did better than my father" (who in turn did better than his) and "My sons and daughters will do even better than I" typify this experience. It is precisely the inapplicability of such statements to underclass people that sets them apart; for most are the sons and daughters of previous generations of the poor, and their children will predictably remain in the grip of poverty. Many members of this class, in fact, can be considered the failures or dropouts of the lower class, persons who because of disability, age, race, or ethnicity have been able to obtain only marginal or part-time work for many years or often no work at all. They formed what were called in the early sixties "pockets of poverty," which were not actually small isolated groups in a temporary condition of want, as the phrase suggests, but the permanent nucleus of a swiftly growing underclass. Harrington (1966) referred to them as the poverty culture population. Its members are not exclusively Blacks or other ethnic minorities, nor are they exclusively city dwellers: They can be found in the isolated mountain valleys of Appalachia and across the rural South. But a disproportionately large number are Black men ranging in age from fourteen through twenty-seven who inhabit the rotting cores of nearly every major city. And these are my subjects—the youngsters with no salable skills and no attachment to any system that might help them advance; the young who at best have access only to low-status jobs and more often are unemployed with no legitimate sources of income. They are the ones often identified as the dropouts and social deviants.

The term *underclass* does not connote moral or ethical unworthiness, nor does it have any other pejorative meaning; it simply describes a relatively new population in industrial society. It is not necessarily culturally deprived, lacking in aspirations, or unmotivated to achieve. Many of the long-term poor, those who have been employed for most of their productive lives but who have never moved from the level of bare subsistence living, are essentially part of the underclass. They try to keep body and soul together and maintain a job, but they remain immobile, part of the static poor. Others who could make this adaptation fail to do so, often preferring to remain unemployed rather than accept a job that demands their involvement for the greater part of each day but provides only the barest minimum of financial reward. They seek other options for economic survival ranging from private entrepreneurial schemes to working the welfare system. Hustling, quasi-legitimate schemes, and outright deviant activity are also alternatives to work. And still there are those who do wish to work but cannot find any meaningful employment. They spend a large part of their time hunting for jobs. They try many different low-level jobs, some seasonal, others part-time, but always for a limited period. They may also seek alternatives for survival, sometimes unemployment insurance or welfare when they can meet the eligibility criteria.

The youth in my study had tried many of the above ways to adapt to underclass confinement but were nevertheless a unique section of the underclass. They were first and foremost young, strong, and physically healthy Black men, who despite their desire to achieve, to become something, and to find a job were at a very early age of fourteen, fifteen, or sixteen well on the way to permanent underclass status. As young inner-city men, and a part of the Black urban experience of the fifties, they responded to their rejection with explosiveness; they used fire to bring a nation to a standstill, forcing it to examine their condition.

How did they arrive in this condition? Are they immobile because they are genetically inferior, mentally impoverished, or lacking in motivation or aspirations as many have claimed? Is it that they are just plain lazy, have no desire to work or hold a job, and just prefer to receive handouts? Any such thesis is an oversimplification, if not a distortion, of the complex relationship between ghetto youth and the traditional institutions of society. Their entrapment into underclass status is clearly affected by many factors, primarily the lack of real opportunities to succeed and the limited alternatives provided by socialization patterns of the inner city. Although the "school of the streets" prepares them for specific and often highly functional roles in that social context, these attributes do not necessarily prepare them to achieve effective roles in mainstream life. And the price they pay for potential entrance into that life is quite extraordinary; for in addition to demanding attributes and capacities different from those acquired in the ghetto, society's institutions systematically block and restrict access by their processes, criteria, and demands.

So much of the ghetto youths' anger and despair arises from contact with mainstream institutions, which, almost imperceptibly and very impersonally, reject them. This rejection, especially by such agencies as the schools, often maims and breaks them; it denies their individuality and integrity. To circumvent these consequences, they seek alternatives; however, many of these devices result in even greater loss and failure. And they need not do so repeatedly in order to become downwardly mobile, since failing in only one institution, and sometimes mere contact with only one social agency, is enough to start the decline. In particular, if the failure-inducing institution is supposed to provide primary socialization, as the schools are, the young men's inability to successfully negotiate this system also impedes their access to the other opportunities and social institutions needed for achievement. For them, the survival behavior that many persons consider destructive is the one great protection they have against a system in which failure is almost assured.

Another major cause of their entrapment has been a gradual alteration in the nation's economic development. In contrast with the mid- forties and fifties, when much of the nation's lower class gained steady employment along with rising incomes and upward mobility, the current period offers lower-class and marginal-income groups a rather bleak future. Because of industry's limited expansion and increased use of technology, rather than people, to improve productivity, entry-level and blue-collar jobs—the traditional means of absorbing new and less experienced works—have dwindled considerably. No substantial change in this trend appears imminent, since industry continues to seek profit through automation, computer technology, and the like. Thus as the need for the vast unskilled work force of earlier periods diminishes, those on the bottom of the ladder become unneeded labor and therefore permanent members of the underclass.

Racism is probably the most basic cause of the underclass condition. Racism in the sixties was different. The "for colored" and "whites only" signs of the thirties and forties had been removed, but the institutions of the country were more completely saturated with covert expressions of racism than ever. The exclusion was carried out now by computers, which ostensibly rejected people on the basis not of "race" but of "social profile." With the economic recession and the lack of lower-class jobs to fall back on, Vietnam and army careers were just about the only escape routes left for poor, vocationally obsolete young Blacks.

Maintenance of the Underclass

Survival as an underclass person is an excruciatingly painful social existence that requires herculean individual effort, guile, wit, and much perseverance. Society, mindful of its articulated humanism, assures that the underclass is maintained in some minimally orderly form. A primary network that performs this function is the program of public welfare. Although initially intended to provide a temporary response to persons in need, welfare has become a conglomeration of services that maintain a large portion of the nation's poor. Organized under categorical, emergency, ongoing, short-term, and many other headings, a vast number of public assistance programs, with little interconnection among them, exist for those who are unfortunate enough to need public help. Because each service carries its own criteria for eligibility and use, all too often discrete requirements prohibit effective use of the broad range of programs or combinations thereof. But since there are not too many alternatives to welfare, the users learn how to manipulate within the gray areas of the programs in order to gain maximum benefits. As a result, a veritable state of war exists between poor recipients and distributors of services. This conflict is also acted out in the nation's legislative politics involving congressmen, governors, other city officials, and the poor and their representatives.

Through continuous periodic administrative manipulations—free food stamps, no food stamps, rebates, supplemental benefits, noneligibility rules, increments in payment, alterations in services available—the welfare system makes adjustment to the demands of the needy populations. But these changes do not encourage or provide the means to mobility or to a secure working status; they rather maintain the status of the poor, often punishing those with incentive and serving as a system to monitor parts of the underclass.

The welfare system has grown immeasurably since 1935, when the federal government made its second major effort to aid the poor by enacting the Social Security Act. (The first large-scale federal welfare program was the Freedmen's Bureau of Reconstruction, established in 1865 to provide health care, education, and political participation for disenfranchised, war-torn, and poor Blacks and whites.) From 1937 to 1978, the welfare portion of the national budget has grown from approximately $146.9 million to $25 billion. And the entrapped poor increasingly constitute a permanent part of the entire welfare populations serviced each year. Still there is a group of the poor that is not able to obtain the services of welfare in any helpful proportion, and these are discussed as part of this study group in a later chapter.

The second system that serves to maintain and contain the underclass population is the network of law enforcement agencies, particularly in the inner city—courts, prisons, parole boards, local police, and various inner-city law enforcement agencies, some with social rehabilitation programs including drug and alcohol prevention. Although widely purported to be redirective, this network rarely provides justice or rehabilitation for this population; rather, it becomes a network through which young Blacks cycle, from one program to another, through the proverbial revolving door. Even though precise statistics are hard to come by, it is widely known than young Blacks constitute the disproportionately largest single group incarcerated in the state penitentiaries and other penal institutions across the country. The practice of institutionalizing young Black children and youth extends beyond criminal justice facilities. The director of the Children's Defense Fund recently noted that "among institutionalized children under eighteen—not in criminal or juvenile delinquent facilities—black males are institutionalized at rates more than 70 percent higher than white males; black females at a rate more than 25 percent higher than white females" (Edelman, 1979, p. 47).

A third maintenance system is composed of the health and social services, particularly the notoriously overcrowded, inadequately staffed and managed county and city hospitals. Recently, these have been buttressed by Medicaid—a worthy effort that has unfortunately become a bungling, corrupt bureaucracy increasing the hardship and discomfort of the poor who seek health care. This network is augmented by private and public employment agencies, offering a limited number of seasonal, part-time, or unskilled jobs to those of the working poor and underclass who seek jobs. The common feature of these networks is that little, if any, of what they do helps the users gain significant security, upward mobility, or access to new opportunities.

Maintaining the underclass is clearly expensive, both monetarily and socially; all the major maintenance systems are supported by tax dollars, not only from business but from all classes of wage earners, particularly middle-income workers, who pay an inequitably large share of the cost. Less obvious but very important are the damaging effects on the Black community that these systems have, making those served less self-sufficient while perpetuating the permanence of this subgroup. Paradoxically, although the Black community has more professionals and skilled workers and a broader range of expertise than ever before, it remains vulnerable to the growth of the underclass.

Working Blacks who cannot afford to support the underclass group or disentangle themselves by moving to new residences remain in the inner cities and in close proximity to the underclass. In this situation, Blacks with somewhat more stable incomes become prey to the trapped underclass youth, who eke out their existence by hustling and ripping off their neighbors.

Middle-income Blacks are also aware of the underclass impact on community life. Some seek relief through flight to suburbia. But wherever they live, because all Black life is in some ways intrinsically bound together—whether through the church one attends, maintenance of family ties and old neighborhood friendships, or the necessary use of community institutions—contact with the underclass is almost inevitable. Still others try to escape by becoming absorbed in mainstream institutions and life. Yet a growing number maintain in-city residence, refusing to seek relief through flight. Although the class of educated Blacks—professionals, administrators, managers, technologists, urbanologists, engineers, and others—has the ability to respond more effectively to community needs, its members are usually busy meeting the demands of their professional roles and of mainstream life. And, as a result, their expert knowledge has been little used to treat the ills of the Black community itself. Even though the more recent growth of the Black middle-income group has in large measure been the consequence of the social upheavals of the 1960s, their involvement in mainstream activities nearly eliminates their ability and, in some cases, desire to attend to the crisis of the underclass.

Forced each day into different milieus for their livelihood, underclass and middle-income Blacks in most cases fail to have positive social contacts. They remain organizationally separated, yet each group pursues survival with vigor—the underclass searches for a way, a hustle, some means to maintain itself; the middle-income group seeks to at least make secure its second-class middle classness. Thus the dialogue prevailing between Blacks of all classes in the sixties has begun to wane in the seventies, and the underclass in its isolation threatens whatever small gains the working and middle-income population achieves, and intracommunity restlessness and antagonism is ever increasing. The continuous growth and confinement of a permanent underclass within the community signals the depth of the socioeconomic crisis faced by Blacks in the eighties. Inattention to the underclass represents the single greatest danger to maintaining a healthy cohesive Black community.

2

Research in a
Black Community

The primary purpose of this research was to gain knowledge about what happened with the young Black urban dwellers in the sixties who have become the large-scale failures of the seventies. That is, what factors in their sociocultural experience negatively affect their achievement of viable life goals; why do they become early dropouts from school, hold no secure jobs, or achieve no social mobility? In spite of all manner of explanatory theory and intervention strategy, why do so many inner-city Black males fail to negotiate the system, and why is this pattern of failure so widespread? As a way of examining this question, I chose to test the poverty culture thesis by determining whether young working-class and low-income Black males do in fact aspire to social and economic mobility and, if they do, what is the nature and scope of those desires. How motivated are they to strive for their goals? What means do they use to advance themselves and to secure satisfying roles? What are the obstacles to success as they perceive them? How do they adapt to failure? A number of related questions pertained to the context of their aspirations and striving—that is, do they consider mainstream society or Black culture as the best area for fulfilling their aspirations? For instance, do they need different attitudes and behaviors to advance in the two settings? What kinds of achievement are possible in each? Do the consequences of failure in these settings differ? In which milieu did they see greater opportunity, and therefore in which one were they more likely to seek achievement? The study was also designed to ascertain their views concerning various models of success, both middle-class Blacks who had advanced along conventional paths and Black achievers who had gained their status more independently. Since upward mobility for most Blacks still means moving into a different culture, I explored with them what they thought about the demands faced by the various Black social classes.

Within this context, the cultural deprivation concept was also tested by examining in a more general way the psychological makeup, attitudes, beliefs, and behaviors of ghetto youth. Here emphasis was on their social behavior and the socialization processes that produced it. Included were investigations of communication styles ("rapping"); special kinds of social gatherings and their attendant rituals; the relationships between males and between men and women; and, perhaps most important, their experience with and adaptations to the mainstream institutions in their lives. The questions here were whether their behavior is effective in meeting their survival needs and whether it also helps them handle the tasks of personal development, planning, and building in an urban industrial society. To gain insight into these last questions, I sought information on the efficacy of the strategies they used to change their condition, ranging from confrontation (for example, what roles had they played in the 1965 rebellion and what reasons did they give for their involvement) to participation in reform efforts and the creation of programs of independent development.

The broadest category of goals included documentation of the history and character of ghetto life, particularly as exemplified by Watts. The major purpose here was to analyze how the mainstream agencies and externally controlled systems that operate in the inner city affect the behavior—the aspirations, adaptations, and ultimately the mobility—of young lower-class men. Overall, my intention was to examine urban ghetto life from the point of view of the actors and to look at their behavior as objectively as possible, without assuming at the outset, as is usually done, that it is deviant or valueless.

The major research, which was supported by a grant from the National Institute of Mental Health, began in 1965 shortly before the Watts rebellion. It continued for three years, with collection of follow-up data in 1975. The subjects were a group of males, aged fourteen to thirty-four, who were considered some of the most incorrigible young people in Watts. The population studied represented about one third of a group of approximately ninety young men who each day gathered outside of a low-income project in an area called the "Parking Lot." Most of these men experienced the greater portion of their young lives in Watts. Some were born there, while others migrated there in the fifties; most attended Watts' schools and all were residents. They had in common the characteristic of being from low-income families, and they too remained poor, receiving almost no income from regular employment. These young men had terminated school early and were identified by almost every social agency as hardcore problems.

Theoretical Background

Only about a decade earlier, I was being raised in the northeastern ghetto of Bedford-Stuyvesant in Brooklyn and thus was especially sympathetic to and interested in the plight of the young Watts dwellers. I wanted to find out how they survived in that environment in the plush times of the fifties and sixties, what roles they aspired to, and how they adapted to this task and to failure and rejection. Attempts to scientifically analyze these questions presented some formidable problems. For the first step, review of the literature on these and related subjects showed that much of what had been written was at great variance with my own experience as a male child in a poor working-class family (which also strove to overcome poverty and social restrictions to achievement). Aside from many questionable assumptions, a basic problem was that the literature lacked the ethnic perspective of a participant in the experience.

In short, much of the material was one-sided and without sensitivity to ghetto life.

A persistent weakness of earlier research is its failure to examine the aspirations and goal-striving patterns of ghetto youth and to measure these in relation to the social and political ambitions and the real opportunities available to Blacks as a whole. Because of this failure, the study of the poor working-class or low-income Black experience has been dominated by two major approaches: (1) comparative analyses of Blacks and whites, and (2) examinations of the life-styles of lower-class people, considered as a unique (usually especially exotic or deviant) subculture (McCord and others, 1969). The first approach has provided the rationale for mainstream exclusion of Blacks, since comparison studies have overwhelmingly found Blacks to be less able to meet mainstream standards of performances than a presumably comparable group of whites. The second approach more or less follows from the first, in that ghetto youths' lack of preparation and demonstrated capacity is ascribed to their special social experience of poverty and cultural deprivation.

Much of the Black-white comparative research has been organized under the general rubric of race relations and has been undertaken by white researchers who assume that the only real alternative to underclass life is integration into white society. Consequently, they have been concerned with such questions as: How much have Blacks moved away from their ethnic, "soulful" ways and have assimilated the dominant society culture? How many are ready to gain access? What should be done to change the behavior of those who are not ready? In essence, what is the nature and scope of the modifications that Blacks have to make for white society to comfortably accommodate their presence? Thus change strategies based on this point of view become gradualist and accommodative. And although strategies contend that change will occur, that openings will be made in the mainstream when Blacks show the necessary readiness, what in large measure really determines Blacks' entrance into mainstream life is whether the majority is ready to accept them and, more recently, whether real roles are available in mainstream structure. The onus obviously rests on the Black to become worthy. The true impact of institutional barriers and racism is denied or ignored, and stress is placed instead on altering or "improving" individual behavior that is considered dysfunctional.

As mentioned earlier, the Black perspective is missing from most research in this area. Ghetto life is thought to be either a rather unimportant transitional state or a serious handicap. The positive side—the great intelligence and skill that ghetto youths demonstrate in coping with their environment—is seldom acknowledged. Race relations analysts also neglect the fact that for young urbanized people (and for that matter the working masses of Blacks) mainstream culture is not necessarily the center of their orientation. Ghetto youth relate principally to their daily environment, and much of their socialization is geared to surviving in that context. Entering the mainstream is only a chance alternative, one demanding totally different kinds of behavior and attitudes. Furthermore, even when researchers examine the mobility strivings of young Blacks in relation to the broader middle-class society, they often omit a critical assessment of underclass youths' opinions of the Black middle class. These analysts assume that the young ghetto dwellers uncritically look upon their more affluent brothers as success models. In reality, their attitudes are quite ambivalent and complex, as we shall see later.

Suffice it to say here that no sound evaluation of any group of Blacks can be done without relating it to what is available for all in Black life. This means that the behavior and aspirations of ghetto youth must be compared with those of Blacks of other social classes. Such comparative studies could reveal whether underclass striving behavior and aspirations are different from those of other Black strivers or are different only from those standardized ones expected by the mainstream. Further, carefully designed studies could shed light on whether or not there are some new variables in the mobility search that did not exist for earlier strivers. Such research is clearly needed, particularly in light of the more recent debate in Black circles concerning whether class or race is the crucial factor effecting Black underachievement (see Wilson, 1978). In the end, such a focus may help disclose whether young inner-city dwellers are not adequately prepared or are just plain unwilling to follow the paths to achievement taken by previous generations.

The aspirations of the ghetto residents should also be examined in relation to the history of Blacks' striving for advancement and equality. The literature on this subject reveals two main currents. The first stresses the development of independence and Black self-reliance, as exemplified by the Garvey Movement, the Black Muslims, and such self-help groups as the Father Divine Movement in the early thirties. This point of view has been articulated by Martin Delany, Malcolm X, and W. E. B. Dubois, among others. The other current, the one with which today's generation is more familiar, emphasizes assimilative activity. Its spokesmen have included Booker T. Washington, Paul Robeson, Roy Wilkins, Whitney Young, and many others (see Cruse, 1967). The civil rights movement of the 1960s represented the crest of this social action wave, as Black and white citizens joined in trying to make integration a reality. But whether these movements were "nationalistic" or "integrationist," all sought in one form or another to advance the rights of Blacks and to create new opportunities for a better quality of life; no significant movement, however militant, sought to reverse the condition of racism by imposing Black domination on whites. The strategies adopted by most of the movements were framed around two major foci: (1) to operationalize an already articulated national, moral, ethical, or political creed, or (2) to stimulate broader society to undertake a new action to improve the condition of Blacks.

Since ghetto youth, whether urban or rural, are always aware of the aspirations, demands, and activities of the larger Black society, they are bound to be affected by the various currents swirling around them. Being politically and socially aware is normal for Blacks, since politicalization is an integral part of socialization for survival in racist surroundings. In 1965, the young men of Watts were no less conscious of "what's happenin'" than earlier generations; in fact, they may have been even more alert than most social analysts had dared to believe. Thus my study looked upon them as part of a social movement, not as an isolated or deviant group. In the end, as discussed in Chapter Eight, they proved to be a vital catalyst in Black community activity and perspective setting.

Another body of literature that affected my research dealt with the broad subject of adaptation or the lack of it. Although this topic has been touched upon earlier, it is worth looking at again as a whole since it pretends to speak about psychobehavioral dynamics. This body of literature examines the Black experience in white America, and suggests that certain predominant behavioral characteristics have been developed by Blacks in response to this experience. The community of Blacks is said to represent a cultural system paralleling the broader American cultural system but providing a uniquely different experience. This dual existence, being a part of and separate from the broader society, derives from Blacks not being allowed to compete on equal terms with the whole of American society (Pettigrew, 1964). Related research provided evidence of the unique stresses this experience produces, with special attention to upwardly mobile Blacks, who exist marginally and feel a kind of "double alienation": They must often curtail their cultural ties when they enter the standard paths to achievement, yet they still are not allowed full access to the new social context (Derbyshire and Brody, 1964).

Other literature goes further to suggest that certain predominant behavioral characteristics were developed by Blacks in response to their unique position in racially divided America. They offer the notion of a "Negro personality," in which special psychological or attitudinal configurations are dominant. These special coping and adaptive patterns that emphasized suspicion, fear of relatedness, mistrust, problem of control of aggression, the denial mechanism, and a tendency to dissipate the tension of a provocative situation by reducing it to something simpler or entirely different were thought to result in a "mark of oppression"—that is, a Black personality (Kardiner and Ovessey, 1964; Karon, 1964). Although varying in some minor detail, these and various other works are dominated by a consistent perception that Black behavior is governed by a negative and therefore a self-debilitating psychology. They support the belief that Black underachievement is primarily self-generated. There is a noticeable absence of authors who see the importance of Blacks' determination to maintain a community. The Black community is most often viewed as a negative or reactionary development. Hence researchers do not consider any real positives to be derived from this existence. On the whole, therefore, they see self-debilitating, negative, and impeding psychological measures being adapted by Blacks. More recently, works conceptualized under a similar framework (that is, believing that a person's behavior is influenced and affected by his social experience) have begun to question this one-sided body of knowledge. They agree with the specialness of the Black experience in white America, but they have also offered findings that speak to the strength of the Black personality and the family and the strength afforded by the Black community (Grier and Cobbs, 1968; Hill, 1972; Valentine, 1968).

Another explanation offered for ghetto youths' failure to adapt to and succeed in the dominant society is the "culture shock" or "culture lag" theory (Wilson and Lantz, 1957). Essentially, its proponents suggest that coming to America from a distinctly different way of life made it difficult for people with African ancestry to adjust to their new milieu. Less simple but more popular today is the "culture of poverty" thesis. Advocates of this view hold that inner-city Blacks have individual deficiencies resulting from a defective cultural experience that produces poor motivation, low aspirations, ignorance, backwardness, underdeveloped social skills, and psychological handicaps (often manifested as self-hatred). This thesis has grown out of the reality that there are commonalities in underclass lifestyles, which are visible wherever such people congregate. Support for this theory is also based on the widespread observed failure of poor and low-income Blacks to achieve in mainstream pursuits. All one has to do is look in any dark ghetto and one will find a common language (understandable to most Blacks), similar ways of associating with friends and family members,

and common institutions—churches, social groups, family structures—with almost identical procedures and social norms.

Nevertheless, the questions remain: Why are these patterns
found in such widely separated areas? How is this culture transmitted? Is this unconsciously transported, like a disease, from
one human carrier to another, from one ghetto to another? Is
this possible when many persons in one ghetto have had little or
no contact with those in other, far-off enclaves? One answer offered by sociology is that the poverty culture is handed down
by Black social and cultural institutions, principally the family
(Rainwater and Yancey, 1967). But despite a number of other
possible ways to think about this issue, almost no researcher has
suggested that some common structures in the American experience to which Blacks, and especially poor Blacks, are continually
exposed are instrumental in shaping this shared culture (Clark,
1965). These structures, which include the schools and law-
enforcement networks cited earlier and which function much
the same across the country, ultimately elicit similar responses
from ghetto youth. They develop a relatively common set of
reactive behaviors, attitudes, and psychological sets to deal with
their rejection and confinement, as well as shared beliefs regarding the broader society, its function, and its objectives with respect to them as Blacks. These beliefs are reinforced each day
by their encounters with the representatives of the mainstream
and its institutions.

Behaviors of young inner-city Blacks are not randomly
transmitted however; they are consciously propagated via special socialization rituals that help the young Blacks prepare for
inequality at a very early age. With maturity, these modes of behavior are employed to neutralize the personally destructive effects of institutionalized racism. Thus, they form the basis of
a "survival culture" that is significantly different from the so-
called culture of poverty. Notwithstanding its reactive origin,
survival culture is not a passive adaptation to encapsulation but
a very active—at times devious, innovative, and extremely resistive—response to rejection and destruction. It is useful and necessary to young Blacks in their present situation; yet there is

some question whether this adaptive style will help them meet the demands they may encounter when oppressiveness is finally thrown off or if they gain opportunities for independent development.

Methodological Problems

The nature of such a study population as the one in Watts makes exceptional demands on the investigator. He needs at least some knowledge of Black history, an awareness of the social and political conditions of Black life in the sixties, and considerable familiarity with ghetto dwellers' culture and language. The researcher also must be flexible, willing to adopt innovative procedures that will respond to the exigencies of the situation without distorting the data. And he has to take on the difficult double role of data collector and participant observer. Because of such requirements, I found research in Watts quite taxing yet, in the end, extremely gratifying.

Just gaining entry to the study group was the first hurdle. This was made possible through the efforts of Billy J. Tidwell, a social worker of an agency called Special Services for Groups (SSG); the fact that he had been born and raised in Watts was a great advantage. The next task was to earn the group's trust, not easy either because there was great unrest among ghetto youth at that time; police surveillance was at a saturation point, the communities of Blacks and whites were sharply polarized, and lower-class Blacks generally distrusted any agencies, programs, and representatives of the dominant culture. In such an atmosphere researchers were not welcome, either because they were suspected of being police or other outside agents or because their ability to express a "Black" view was questioned.

When I commenced the study, I had frankly begun with some rather standardized notions and preconceptions about how I would go about it. I soon discovered that my conventional, fixed interview schedule would be impossible to adhere to. This quickly forced me to adopt methods of study appropriate to the situation. For one thing, I found that I could rarely do a seated interview; work done literally on the run was common.

And it was not unusual for respondents to disappear—they had been jailed or had left the community for reasons of survival. I just had to wait and hope that when, and if, they reappeared they would feel as open to me as they had before; sometimes the incarceration or "ducking" had so stimulated their paranoia that voluntary giving of information was out of the question. Under these conditions, it could take two to three months to complete the interview and was often a considerable accomplishment.

Furthermore, I soon learned that being able to hold an interview with one subject at a time or in private was rare. Most interviews were conducted in the day-room of their organization, the Sons of Watts (described in Chapter Eight). Very often the interviewee would call on his friends to confirm his judgments or statements and would even use them as a vehicle to rap the responses. The friends received approval to add their own nuances and factual clarifications, and they would usually confirm or expand on the initial response. These interviewing conditions had some important benefits: they allowed the group members to confirm, particularly at the beginning of the study, that I was seeking the same information from each person; no one subject was receiving special attention by being asked different questions that could then be used against him. In the end, the procedure permitted a more natural flow of communication consistent with the pattern of these men's life-styles.

Thus an "open" interview was developed. And although interviewing in a group setting did have its positive side—it legitimized the researcher's function as "recorder" of events—I had to take special care to differentiate the inputs of the primary respondent from those of the group members. The inability to use a tape recorder, as originally planned, made data collections somewhat more tedious and also prohibited content analysis of the data. Nonetheless, the comfort the group gained by this action paid off in the subsequent openness with which those data were given.

More important than the change in the interviewing methods, however, was my decision to be a participant observer. Because of my subjects' attitudes toward research and my own desire to capture the essence of their experience as completely as possible, this role became an appropriate one, and my early upbringing allowed me to adapt to it relatively quickly. Some may assert, however, that my involvement may have adversely affected the validity of the research, that the study should have been undertaken by someone who brought no bias to the examination. But one of the fallacies of social science is that there is such a thing as "no bias." Without doubt, my past had some bearing on what was observed and what issues were deemed important. Yet this would be equally true for any other investigator, white or Black. The criticism of research lodged by Blacks is that so much of it is done by whites, and that white bias and perspective have framed the issues to be studied and determined the ways the findings have been presented.

The view that the researcher who maintains distance and detachment will produce more "objective" evidence is derived from a wish to emulate physical science. However, the study of human behavior precludes the objectivity that the hard sciences presumably attain; bias is always present to some degree. Thus, my past experiences did not, in my view, weaken the investigation but may have added to the authenticity of the observations. Young social researchers in the 1960s shared this conviction and tried to use the inevitable involvement of the investigator for positive ends, arguing that greater identification and empathy with the population being studied are needed to fully grasp its character.

Necessity also enters into the choice of the participant observer role. More recent research with Blacks, particularly underclass Blacks, has disclosed that all who function in this milieu must interact in some way. There are no long-standing pure observers; everyone is either a participant or a potential target. Even the researcher, despite the special status that may be accorded him, is still subject to being "hit on." Thus out of need, if not out of commitment, the researcher becomes involved in the movement, the cadence, of street life. If he is to survive there, he must often be part of the action.

At the same time, of course, he cannot allow himself to be engulfed completely. He must be alert and able to observe both positive and negative aspects of unfolding data, and must make sure that he is not so involved that his presence might substantially distort the natural processes of the study group. For example, it is one thing to participate in a social custom such as "sucking on wine" and quite another to mount the podium and lead a rap session vilifying the "honky devil." In fact, underclass youth are not much beguiled by the conspicuously demonstrative Establishment brother, the professional who makes a show of being more radical than the truly poor and ghetto-bound Black. They know that shortly after he "blows" he will climb into his "GTO, heading for the hill to relax behind some scotch in his air-conditioned crib." Besides not fooling his study group, the researcher who has to act out for them is definitely an active catalyst of events, rather than a recorder and systematic collector of data.

Disciplined reserve is often the most difficult part of this role; for social oppressiveness and racism have no less an impact on the Black researcher than on the study population. In this case, the racially oppressive character of Watts was very vivid, since it replicated what I had experienced as a poor Black male in the streets of Bedford-Stuyvesant. It was hard to be detached when I watched these young men respond to system rejection, dragnets, roustings, and the many other indignities they faced each day. Above all else, I was captured emotionally by the marvelous skills they employed to gain gratification and, most important, to survive. Yet as mentioned earlier, I had to acknowledge that those very skills—such as quick, innovative reactions to situations—might have little utility for life tasks requiring planning and perseverance.

In short, the researcher must strike a balance, neither too distant nor too involved. If the participant observer can manage to be aware of his own needs and feelings while recognizing the demands and reality of the study group, he can add a significant dimension to the research. For as an insider, he is able to home in on an issue and examine the data in ways that the investigator who approaches from the outside cannot.

Another matter that arises in studies of Blacks by Blacks is language. How are the screened and coded messages with which

Black speech is saturated to be dealt with? Researchers unfamiliar with ghetto language have for a long time received such messages, often without awareness of their complicated meanings;
they may be misled or may understand the words but miss the
essential meaning because their roots and experiences are different from those of the study group. The researcher with a shared
background is in a better position to unravel the communication, but still it is often a ticklish business. He must decide when
he should rely on his experience to get the meaning and when
he can risk asking the speaker to clarify himself. If the researcher
asks too many questions, he may indicate that despite his Black
skin he is not really a "brother" but instead an alien who does
not understand. For example, certain expressions that form almost a refrain, such as "Can you dig?" and "Like, you know,
that's what's happening," leave the receiver responsible for obtaining the real message. "Can you dig?" does not really invite
the receiver's questioning for clarity, and "Like that's what's
happening" even more assumes a perfect harmony between
speaker and listener. Although making the communication clear
is obviously important in securing reliable data, it may be more
important in some cases to remain temporarily in doubt rather
than lose the confidence of the population. In my role, I tried
to maintain a posture of critical questioning, as opposed to in-
quisitive seeking. Whenever it became possible, I asked to have
these common expressions clarified, because I wanted the
speakers to take more responsibility for explaining their meaning.

The speech of these young men is obviously an important
means to understanding their experience. Therefore I have presented it verbatim or paraphrased it throughout this book. To
retain its vividness and to avoid distortion, I have usually not
translated it into standard English or the language of social
science. Some readers may be mystified occasionally, but I think
the argot is comprehensible in most cases.

3

IIIIIIIIIIIIIIIIIIIIIIIIIIIIIIIIIIIIIIIIIIIIIIIIIIIIIIIIIIIIIIIIIIIIIIIIIIIIIIIIIIIIIIIIIIIIII

Defining a
Black Ghetto

IIIIIIIIIIIIIIIIIIIIIIIIIIIIIIIIIIIIIIIIIIIIIIIIIIIIIIIIIIIIIIIIIIIIIIIIIIIIIIIIIIIIIIIIIIIIII

In this country Blacks as a group represent the have-nots, whites the haves. The conflict between the two, although it has shifted from the open confrontations of the sixties, remains constant. Today it is manifested in the struggle to control the political processes, the jobs, the educational institutions, the limited housing and the better residential areas, and even the good-quality food. Although the two groups tacitly agreed to re-linquish open confrontation after the upheavals of the sixties, tension is once again mounting in the cities, this time caused by the return of those whites who have abandoned suburban living and are now seeking residences in the inner cities.

City governments are doing little to alleviate the conflict. Despite the efforts of a few concerned urbanologists, social planners, and community developers, the fight for space, for housing, and for city-related jobs continues to be waged with-out adequate municipal involvement. Urban governments have failed to develop careful policies controlling land acquisition by private investors; they have offered builders few incentives to construct low-income housing; and they have not encouraged social agencies to participate in developing "neighborhoods" and

31

balanced communities—these are but a few of the factors that combine to create a pattern of city living in which Blacks and whites, low-income and middle-income folk, compete for advantage. In such a situation, the poorest and most powerless Blacks and other minorities become the consistent losers, displaced from their city dwellings. Since these communities are usually stratified by race and income, their housing patterns reflect the social pattern of separation and inequality.

It is not difficult to understand why Black Americans become enraged when asked by seemingly intelligent mainstreamers, "How come Negroes continue to live the way they do?" Referring to their progress, white Americans say, "We made it and we lived in slums when we first came to this country. Why don't colored people have entrepreneurial aspirations? They're not business-minded. How come they want to move up so fast? It took us years to attain what we have." The questions go on *ad infinitum*, while the answers remain right out in the open, not hidden from anyone.

The cities' decay is not due primarily to Black occupancy per se, but to past white flight and the attitudes mainstream institutions adopted toward the cities once the large population of whites had departed. As Blacks inherited the cities and came to fit the typology "Chocolate City," businesses left, social services deteriorated, good consumer products and supermarkets became less available, the tax base of earlier periods declined, insurance rates skyrocketed, bank loans for property improvement or maintenance became scarce or unavailable, and all manner of erosion was allowed to occur. As a result of local government policies of inattention, many cities now face bankruptcy and collapse.

The problems of separated living are not new; they are only more consolidated and more dramatic. Over time a number of factors have contributed to the pattern of Blacks living in the nation's cities. First, the migration of Blacks from the rural south in the post-Civil War reconstruction, again in the twenties and in larger numbers in the forties in search of jobs and some measure of equal opportunity early established the urban area as the locale for residence (Drake and Cayton, 1970). Despite this migration, more than 52 percent of Blacks still live in the South. Notwithstanding, a significant Black population can be found in almost every metropolis in the nation and living in areas separated from whites. In fact, in at least eighty cities, Blacks constitute the majority, often living close to large industrial centers where blue-collar work provides the major source of family income (Kerner, 1968).

A second factor, referred to in Chapter One, is the consolidation of areas within the city as "dark ghettos," in which Blacks are confined and maintained. Although urbanologists like to speak of these areas as "low-income" communities of "transition" or "entry," they have in fact become permanent enclaves for a large portion of Blacks (Clark, 1965).

Third, unlike lower-income and upper-income whites, who usually live in distinctly different neighborhoods, separated as an expression of social means and opportunity, Blacks of all income levels live in closer proximity in bounded areas of living. This fact contributes to the greater cohesiveness and sense of "Black community" as articulated by Blacks. It also means that what occurs to one section of the community has an immediate and widespread impact on all members of the community irrespective of income, social status, or differences accorded to individuals by their achievement.

Another pattern of Black living and a contributor to the condition of the cities is the characteristic way that Black living areas grow. Black residences have traditionally been limited to certain sections of the city. As the population of Blacks increases from births and further in-migration, overcrowding ultimately forces more and more inhabitants to search for new living space. Since Blacks do not have access to many residential areas, the ghetto expands from the sheer force of overpopulation and limited resources in the inner core. Poorer and inner-core Blacks remain in central ghetto lower-income areas, and Blacks with some means (particularly with regular incomes), search for housing closer to the periphery of the original core. Whites in bordering communities evacuate toward more distant suburbs. Thus through social expansion a small area becomes enlarged as contiguous residential areas fall to Black habitation.

A somewhat different variation of the social expansion pattern of growth is sometimes created by middle-income Blacks and some families with lower but consistent incomes who manage to secure housing somewhat beyond the immediate borders of the ghetto; they integrate white communities. However, shortly afterward these outskirt communities, called "gilded ghettos," also become linked to the Black central area, as whites who are located in the corridor depart and other Blacks, seeing the possibility of gaining housing, start to fill the gap.

A final factor affecting Black living patterns is the more recent reentry of young whites into the central city. Increasingly, whites have secured inner-city residences through reclamation or purchase of property for their habitation. Despite some attempts by lower-income Blacks to organize and resist this influx, urban renewal, available bank loans, and the potential of significant capital gain from property sales has resulted in parts of the inner city undergoing significant racial change from Black to white. Forecasters foresee important changes occurring in relocation of low-income Blacks in the early eighties. Other changes may also be identifiable, particularly the trend of younger Blacks returning to the South. Not all of these factors are new, but it seems clear that the common dynamic of racism and economics, just as it was the basis for the development of the dark ghetto to begin with, continues to dominate to keep Blacks socially separated from mainstream society and to maintain their "second classness."

From Slum to Ghetto

As is well known, the term *slum* denotes a congested area of a city characterized by low-income inhabitants, bad housing, and generally poor living conditions. In the United States, most early slum residents were European immigrants who settled in areas that were ethnically or religiously compatible. The slum as a social structure has been written about and experienced by a large section of today's affluent Americans. In fact, it is even recalled nostalgically by many (Riis, 1968). Undoubtedly their attitudes would be different, however, if the system had not allowed them in. Whatever they suffered, for most of these immigrants the slums were primarily communities of transition and acculturation, preparation for participation in American society. Their belief in mobility was supported by the reality of its occurrence.

So it was precisely the fulfillment of aspirations and the successful transition that distinguished the Europeans' experience of slum living in the thirties from the Blacks' experience of ghetto living in the fifties and sixties. One of the keys to their success was an expanding economy's need for new workers. Another important ingredient was that most slum-based institutions, particularly schools and social welfare organizations, were oriented to help the immigrant attain the tools necessary for mobility. For example, the neighborhood educational institutions concentrated on providing English-language skills, redefining the practice of national customs, and, where necessary, developing job skills. This last task was much simpler than it is today, because industry was not so highly specialized, and the war economy of the forties had the need and the room for semi-skilled and unskilled labor.

Early immigrants not only entered a growing job market, but they also sought control over special vocational and work areas—the Italians ruled the shipyards, the docks, and the teamsters; the Jews took over the garment industry; the Irish, the Germans, and other groups each gained unique provinces of economic control. These work-connected areas provided income and jobs for group members and supported increased group mobility. Control of these economic provinces also supported greater intragroup dependency and increased the interdependence and accountability of members of ethnic, national, and religious communities.

Although some slums still show evidence of their former ethnic character, most of the earlier inhabitants have completely abandoned them. When one immigrant group left, another replaced it, a transition that took an average of two .generations to complete. The process was expedited by economic opportunity and by the supportive social institutions, but probably the most significant element was the immigrants' race. Because they were white, they could easily blend into the dominant Caucasian society, which was receptive to absorbing them.

In contrast, the movement of Blacks into some of these very same slums had very different characteristics. The first and most profound difference was that the large majority who migrated to the city were citizens of the United States. Rather than being recent arrivals from foreign shores, bringing alien traditions, customs, and languages, most were from the rural South and had a two-hundred-year heritage in the United States. Later they in-migrated to various parts of the country. Second, they were Black, the descendants of African ancestors, most of whom had arrived involuntarily as slave laborers. Thus they were different not only in having dark skin but in carrying the historical mark of enslavement.

A further alleged distinction between Black and immigrant dwellers concerns their entrepreneurial skills. Blacks' lack of mobility has often been ascribed to the lack of such skills. And in some cases it is true that white immigrant groups had greater experience of this kind, particularly those, such as Jewish immigrants, who had already accumulated much mercantile and business experience before their trek to America. However, the lack of skill was not an important variable distinguishing Blacks from some Poles, Irish, and groups from southern Europe such as Italians. These groups came with desire and aspiration, from poverty, disadvantage, and often socioeconomic failure, to a society that saw fit to absorb them with limited cultural modification. Indeed, they were unskilled, but, more important, they were Caucasians. As a consequence, principally of race, then, what was initially a slum became a ghetto for all classes of Blacks. The dark ghettos expanded to accommodate an increased population of Blacks; by 1967 a congressional committee found that American institutions had created, maintained, and condoned the confinement of Blacks in ghettos (Kerner, 1968).

The Ghettoization of Watts

The city of Los Angeles is a metropolis of approximately seven and a half million people spread over an area of about 454 square miles. The Human Relations Commission of Los Angeles estimated that in 1968 Blacks represented at least 17 percent of the total population. But most of these (85 percent) were compressed in an area covering about 65 square miles. Watts, a small community located ten miles south of the central city, was only one early segment of this large ghetto complex. Although Black men and women of Watts (rarely children) were seen in downtown Los Angeles, the nature of their lives and their community was unknown to most Americans, including Los Angelenos. Many Blacks commuted to jobs in the city, but in the five o'clock rush hour the vehicles headed home in color-differentiated streams: the Blacks south to Adams, Avalon, Willowbrook, and Watts; the whites north and west to the Hollywood Hills, Beverly Hills, Sherman Oaks, and the San Fernando Valley. And there they took up their separate existences, largely ignorant of one another, until the explosion of 1965 forced white America to recognize the plight of Blacks. Watts no longer remained a hidden by-way, but became a symbol of a new explosiveness among Blacks.

The ghettoization of Watts began in the early forties with the advent of the war industries boom. The development of this community as an isolated ghetto was forecast by the American Council on Race Relations as early as 1947. It noted that before World War II the population of Watts was evenly divided among Mexican-Americans, Blacks, and whites. But between 1942 and 1947 a very heavy in-migration of rural and southern Blacks was accompanied by a similar exodus of the other two groups, and by 1947 Blacks made up five sixths of the population. Although a few whites still lived there and others had moved their families but held on to their businesses, the remaining one sixth comprised Latinos, who increasingly came into conflict with Blacks. By 1949, a report noted that:

> Watts is a polygot community bothered by intercultural tensions and insecurities. By day, it is teaming

with Negroes and Mexican-Americans shopping and hanging about the stores of the white merchants. One Hundred and Third Street is the half-world of Los Angeles, and the commuter passing it on his Pacific Electric car from Long Beach sees nothing outstanding about this community *except that it is Negro*. But should he walk around 103rd Street after sundown, pushing through the crowds, clustering about the bars or gathering on sidewalks to watch the wrestling matches on T.V., he would sense a difference. . . . The street lights are small and too far between to be of much help. . . . Fights and occasional killings underline the tension in this area where two minority groups are blindly pitted against each other, each group facing job discrimination, poor housing, and inadequate recreational facilities, with few attempts at intercultural education and understanding [Robinson, 1949; pp. 37–38].

Housing. The way in which this constricted, tension-filled situation developed is typical. With the increased demand for labor occasioned by the war industries, local government planners and business interests could easily forecast the large-scale influx of Blacks seeking economic betterment. The question was, where and in what would they live? Although the usual practice in Los Angeles County was to build one-family homes for newcomers, particularly when the incoming population resulted from new industry and employment, the housing for the new Black workers of Watts took the form of low-cost, two-story projects. These were intended not only to provide inexpensive dwellings for Blacks but to lessen the growing apprehension of whites, who saw Black families searching for places to live in all the neighborhoods close to their employment. The investment in the housing projects also reflected the understanding of housing and business interests that the livable incomes achieved by Blacks in war jobs were, for the most part, only temporary. There is some evidence, too, that Watts had been selected by powerful interests as an area of Black segregation and therefore as an appropriate site for the projects. How ironic that in less than twenty years the low-income housing development would be the hub of incendiary actions against ghetto confinement!

The housing projects did not long succeed in containing Blacks. As the small area of Watts became more densely populated and as Blacks' incomes increased, the search for housing burst into the adjacent communities, in the manner described at the beginning of this chapter. Of course, these communities did not succumb without resistance. In south central Los Angeles, restrictive covenants were openly written and actively supported by whites. The residents of Willowbrook, for instance, "protested vehemently against Negro occupancy, threatening to burn any Negro housing which might be established and to mob any Negroes who might attempt to move in" (Fisher, 1947, p. 11). At a city council meeting, they went on record as saying, "Willowbrook would either stay lily-white or would run with blood" (Fisher, 1947, p. 11). Despite such threats and intimidation, however, Blacks did obtain living space in fringe communities, which then, following the familiar pattern, lost nearly all their white residents. Those with means fled to the suburbs, where they felt they were beyond the reach of Blacks during their lifetime. In the main, the only ones remaining were the old and disabled, abandoned by their younger kin.

Thus does segregated living become a reality. It does not, as has often been contended, result from the free choice of Black citizens who want to live together. Rather, it is a consequence of mainstream activity, bolstered by laws that ultimately support racial prejudices and fears, and more often than not it is exploited for economic gain. Thus as communities change from white to Black, realtors and white property owners reap large profits. Spreading rumors of property and community devaluation, realtors exploit the basic racist fears of the white owners; these whites abandon their urban homes to realtors or other speculators who then double the prices and sell to Blacks, who desperately seek housing. Profits are made by both the former owners and the realtors. Whites who can contain their panic may eliminate the middle man by selling their property themselves. In many cases, however, the profiting does not end there. The seller, encountering the often limited cash of the buyer and the banks' practice of denying Blacks loans as poor risks, forces the buyer to secure a second mortgage at very high interest rates. Incidentally, these contracts often give the seller the first option to repossess the property in case the buyer is unable to meet all financial obligations. Clearly, the Black family that seeks housing outside the ghetto pays a high price for a home in a fringe area that is almost certain to become part of the ghetto. Even if it was a Black middle-class gilded ghetto initially, it will, in reality, become a part of the dark ghetto in a very short time.

Interestingly, an exception to this pattern of community change can be found in a few places where white residents are convinced that the advantages of interracial living and the beauty and conveniences offered by a particular location make it worth the effort to stay and encourage other white families to remain; one example of this pattern developed in Baldwin Hills, a community in the west side of Los Angeles. The Blacks in these areas typically have middle or upper incomes. However, unless there are active procedures to keep Blacks and whites together, almost any urban community having a racial mixture can safely be identified as an area in flux. Heretofore, integrationist-oriented, middle-class Blacks have sought to stabilize interracial living patterns, but this concern is becoming increasingly passe as the basic struggle for land for decent homes for Blacks takes priority.

Schooling. Changes in the institutional structure of the area inhabited by Blacks then begin to occur. The educational system became a part of Watts' development as a ghetto. Despite public utterances by school officials identifying the school system as one of the positive community institutions, the process of preventing great numbers of Black students from entering professional and white-collar careers had begun as early as the forties. This was accomplished principally by devaluing school curriculum. As Fisher (1947, p. 13) reported, "The only high school in Watts, despite the fact that it was interracial in both faculty and students, was being given over virtually exclusively to commercial courses." However, the white students were given special counseling and were encouraged to go elsewhere to school.

Black parents have long been suspicious of the "commercial course" rhetoric. They have been told repeatedly by school counselors and educators about the dignity of manual labor, about the equal status of those who go to college and those who train for vocations. But they know that these counselors are simultaneously ensuring that white youngsters pursue a college-preparatory curriculum, while Black students take dietary science, automotive mechanics, and homemaking. Recognizing that technical skills are important, Blacks nevertheless become weary when commercial education is pushed at them so vigorously, while white students are groomed for professional roles. They find it hard to believe that a system that discriminates and abridges access is really committed to providing solid training for relevant future roles for Blacks.

It is difficult at best to understand all the factors that have contributed to the discrepancies in educational attainment between Blacks and whites. However, one suspects that, in addition to many other factors, the two-track system for differentially directing Black and white students has contributed to the discrepancies found in 1960. Of the adult population of Watts, that is, persons aged twenty-five and over, 32.5 percent had had less than eight years of school and only 9.7 percent had had one or more years of college. In contrast, greater Los Angeles County boasted that it was "above the national average" and that "over half the population twenty-five years of age and over had completed high school . . . and almost 10 percent had completed college or better" (Meeker, 1964).

Economic Structure. Watts' economic character is both a cause and a result of ghettoization. A major problem is that the residents do not control the services, markets, or businesses in their community. The money continually flows out instead of circulating inside. Further, because there are no large industries in Watts, the area has a low tax base and few accessible jobs. Unemployment problems struck the area as soon as the war-related industries of the forties shut down, and they have not lessened. Not only is Watts almost totally devoid of industrial investment, but it remains the area of residence for a large section of the unskilled and semiskilled Black labor force. And, as suggested earlier, their occupational worth and ability to market their labor have decreased as the job market has less and

less need for unskilled labor. Their lack of technical and professional training is compounded by the time-worn practice of
job discrimination. Although its overt forms are less prevalent,
job discrimination still exists, and poverty as the result of unemployment is one index of its seriousness. That Watts is poor
is evident: in 1967, for example, the median annual income was
$4,365.

Thus, in the short period of two decades, the forces that
consolidate a dark ghetto completed their work in Watts. In
1960, a study that compared the incomes, educational achievements, and occupational levels of residents in all Los Angeles
municipalities found that Watts received the lowest possible
score in each category. Of the 124 municipalities studied, only
four others scored as low. Can there be any question why Watts
exploded in 1965? Should we not ask, instead, why it took so
long?

Unique Characteristics of Watts

Though the development of Watts was in many ways typical of ghettos across the country, it was different from its older
counterparts in several significant respects. For one thing, the
surface qualities are much more pleasant. In the Eastern ghettos,
created as long ago as World War I in Harlem, Baltimore, and
Chicago, the sun casts shadows on rows of tightly packed stone
or brick tenements in narrow streets, and snow falls several
months a year. This pattern has been well documented in other
studies (Drake and Cayton, 1970; Sherman 1970; Osofsky,
1966). In the semitropical climate of Watts, the sun shines most
days on small one- or two-family houses surrounded by grass
(these were still characteristic despite the housing projects and
urban renewal apartments built in the sixties and seventies).
Even the lack of heavy, cumbersome clothing adds to the air of
freedom and movement of the California ghetto inhabitants.
And, simply because it is newer, Watts shows less physical wear
than do the intense concrete jungles of the East.

Other differences also have to do with age. The older
Northeastern cities, to which Blacks had migrated for decades,

had by the early twentieth century developed a network of formal institutions, patterns of communication and self-protection
structures, and, most important, a generation of Black citizens
who were knowledgeable about the ways of the city and its
many games. In Watts, no such systems existed at the time the
subjects of this study arrived there. They had few experienced
elders to learn from because most of their own parents had been
reared in rural areas; thus, they represented a first generation of
Blacks in Los Angeles. These immigrants to Watts had to depend
on their individual skill and wit to survive, with little parental
guidance or support from established social organizations. In effect, Watts was not a community, a unit with an identity and
a recognizable structure. It was a sprawling residential area whose
inhabitants had few organizational ties. Those that did exist
were mostly interpersonal ties with relatives and former "down
home" associates. A somewhat limited social rapport with
neighbors or friends developed through community-based social
groups. The absence of community centers, meeting rooms,
dance halls, and the like contributed not only to increased indi-
vidualistic survival behavior but also to particularly loose communication patterns. As a consequence, the street system of information—a central part of ghetto life and protection—was
much less structured in Watts than in the older enclaves. Also
largely absent in Watts were the long-standing, community-
sponsored agencies offering services and help to the new mi-
grants. Some mainstream-supported agencies existed, but even
when they were available, their services often went unused for
a variety of reasons. Some residents felt that they offered irrelevant services, that is, offerings that were unresponsive to their
economic needs, and other residents were uncomfortable using
what they considered alien agencies.

Given a low-level social organization and a lack of strong
political structure, it was predictable that citizen influence and
control of Watts' development would be minimal. Though Watts
had representatives in city and state government, it lacked the
informal network of ties with powerful politicians that existed
in older ghettos. Without these connections, Watts could get
little traditional social action started to deal with its ills. The

failure to develop such a network was due partly to lack of encouragement by local government, which grossly miscalculated the impact that an area of encapsulated Black citizens could have on the workings of a metropolis the size of Los Angeles. But it was also due to the limited political activism during the fifties by poorer Blacks, many of whom lacked real experience in urban politics and who felt that these two parties rarely, if ever, represented their interests. Their dissociation was understandable. Though the Democratic party purported to serve them, their representatives—both whites and mainstream-oriented Blacks—did little to stave off ghettoization. Watts' city council member, for instance, whose job was nonpartisan and whose constituency was heavily Black, was nevertheless a white Democrat until 1951. Billy Mills and Robert Farrell, who were later elected to the city council and represented some of the Watts constituents after the electoral boundaries had been changed, were Black Democrats. Similarly, the state assembly district, which includes areas other than Watts, elected a white Democrat from 1938 to 1961. In 1962, F. Douglas Farrell, a minister born in Texas, became the first Black assemblyman from that district. He was followed by Leon Ralph and currently Maxine Waters, both Black Democrats. Thus, despite the increasing election of Blacks, a not unimportant occurrence, their association with traditional party politics has produced only limited gains, least of all for a growing Watts class of poor. Some residents suggested that an independent political apparatus was needed to focus on Black needs and demands. This type of political development found some limited expression in the mid sixties and was exemplified by social activist groups, such as US and the Black Panthers, but never emerged as a major formalized Black political party. The post-rebellion developments discussed in Chapter Seven provide an example of an attempt to institute needed changes, particularly in the economic sphere.

Watts and the eastern ghettos differ markedly in the composition and density of their populations. In Harlem, for instance, the 60,666 residents at the turn of the century included not only native Blacks but also Blacks of foreign stock and

British backgrounds who had arrived from the various Carib-
bean islands. The latter had their own orientation and psychological makeup, and for long periods the two Black groups con-
flicted. But the common experience of ghettoization and being
closed out of opportunity did a great deal to consolidate them
and minimize intraracial strife. In contrast, those who moved to
Watts were much more homogeneous. Moreover, they were
mostly men looking for work in heavy manufacturing and later
war industry. Their women, when they came, often arrived later,
whereas in the early migrations to New York there were 810
males for every 1,000 females (Glazer and Moynihan, 1967, pp.
25–35). Whatever their gender, however, all these people were
more tightly compacted in the East—in Chicago, Indiana, and in
the Hough Street ghetto in Cleveland, for example—than they
were in the West. Though Watts is a high-density area by Los
Angeles standards, its low concentration in contrast with that of
other enclaves gives it the dangerous illusion of being a normal
suburb.

These differences—the unique structural arrangements,
the associational patterns—certainly affected the events that occurred in August 1965, but, in the final analysis, it was being
poor and Black and seeing no way out of ghetto confinement
that produced the incentive for the Watts uprising.

The Dream and the Reality: 1955 to 1965

In the heat of the evening, on a congested Watts street in
1965, a young man passing by spoke bitterly of the unchanging
condition. He spoke of the "pig" who would jack them up; he
told others and public service workers, "Man, I need a job, I need
to make some money; shit, ain't nothin happenin' out here, just
the same old bullshit—no jobs, no money, no good food—and
the jive-time brothers, and the man, just running games about
what they're trying to do. Shit, we ought to burn this mother,
and rip off some things."

Clearly, the dream with which they and their families had
embarked in the forties and early fifties had failed to materialize. They had not come despairing, angry, and hostile; on the

contrary, sometimes with only a mother or an older sister, a brother or a cousin, they had left southern cities—Galport, New Orleans, Memphis, Jackson, Newelton, Kansas City, Morehead, Arcadia—with aspirations and with fear, but, above all, with hope. They had set out in buses, old cars, and trains for a place of warmth and industry, hoping to leave behind deprivation, discrimination, unemployment, and myriad other troubles. Most came bringing only their youth and a willingness to do the things that they thought would open the doors to a new way of life—a bright, new community; a nice place to live; the possibility of an equal, integrated education, free and public; a job in the city, with employment in something other than agricultural work, in industry if they were lucky, maybe clean work. This was the dream of mobility, of equality; it was the same vision shared by all who migrated north or west.

Even those who were too young to articulate the dream at the time of migration had a definite impression that change for the better would come. For some it was exciting, for others quite frightening. One young man thought back:

> I don't remember too much, but remember hearing the family saying things would be better. I know my mother wanted to go, and I think things weren't so good; you know, hard times, and father wasn't making it. He left first, then we [brother and sister] came after.

Sometimes a family sought a new start away from trouble, and yet the children experienced the move as ripping up their roots.

> I guess the family was pretty glad to get out of there, because my father was in some kind of trouble, so we moved here. I didn't specially want to go; I didn't know what to expect.

And there were those who did not know where they were migrating to, but understood what they were trying to get away from and what they hoped to attain. An unemployed twenty-two-year-old recalled:

I can't remember too much; in a way, I wanted to get away. I was too young to understand the problems then. The house we lived in, you couldn't exactly call it a house; it was two rooms in the back hills. It was hard. My father couldn't make no money there. We had relatives here, so we moved to do better, to see if we could find something.

Almost immediately the dream received some harsh blows. As soon as they arrived, the migrant youngsters had to meet demands for social adjustment. Despite the limited living space and family troubles, Galport at least had the blessings of familiarity—the sounds of the neighborhood, the long-time friendships, the relatives and friends, even the fragrances of familiar food being cooked. The move to the big city, although for some it meant being reunited with relatives or family, presented to almost everyone a strange new environment requiring personal changes. Though these were often quite simple, they had deep impact, as the following comments reveal:

Man, you would never think it, but when I went to school the changes were so great. The other kids took sandwiches, and I wasn't used to that kind of food. Things like tuna fish, and all that other stuff. You know, I felt so bad, I stayed home 'cause I just couldn't eat in school—just wasn't accustomed to it.

By 1950, the dream was beginning to evaporate for most. Watts was already a heavily populated, segregated community floundering in a morass of poverty, which was not always apparent to commuters passing along the main drag, 103rd Street. In 1965, 103rd Street was lined with typical ghetto businesses: small, storefront operations carrying a minimum of low-quality clothing, food, and other merchandise required by the community. The abundantly stocked supermarkets, the large, well-lit gas stations occupying all four corners of intersections, and the blinking "Don't Walk" signs on the street corners, which so epitomize Los Angeles, were absent in Watts. Because so few large, major businesses had invested in this community, the residents did their shopping in adjoining communities when they could.

In central Watts, one watched the children "ditty-bop" out of school, listening to "KGFJ soul." Young people addressed each other on the street: "Say, brother, what's happening?" A group of pitifully young women stood large with pregnancy as their sisters came from school, jiving with the boys who had already begun to develop a style with girls. The men sat on inverted garbage pails, lawns, or automobile fenders, commenting on all the action. They were young, seemingly too young to be unemployed or to have no place to go. The intensity of the streets, the food odors, the sounds of Otis Redding and other wailing Black musicians, the cadence of Black speech and movement—all identified the area as the central ghetto, the Black Boulevard.

One of the older men in the study population, who had come to Watts in 1949, described his Watts of 1967:

> This is like a South Gate, which is an independent patty town. Watts is an independent Negro town. This is a Negro town 99 percent. It should be run by Negroes. The people are mostly laborers, or most of the people are "on county." Ain't too much here, since everyone has to go out to work. The houses are run down; most of the houses are overdue in being ripped down. Look at all the abandoned houses on Hickory Street, just standing barren.

A younger man spoke of the entrapment:

> Watts is an all-Negro community, with some Mexicans. It is a place you live and die in; you never get away. If you leave, you come back.

Others provided a picture of the institutional factors that affected everyone's lives:

> It is a community that needs help. The schooling is not up to par. No housing and no public facilities. Bus lines are poor (only one on Century Boulevard). There is only city ambulance service. Seventy percent of the people who are on jobs find that the money is no good, and allows just enough to feed and house them.

> The housing is not like they are on the West Side. The rents ain't too high, but you have to tell the landlord about roaches and termites. It is a poor neighborhood. The schools don't stress education. The schools can't be any different from the community. The police give a lot of harassment, even if you haven't done nothing. There's a need to clean up the raggedy houses. One good thing is they are building a hospital now, so you won't have to go to General Hospital.

> Watts is a slum area. The people are nice, but the houses need fixing, and there is no top quality food. The canned goods are all bent up. We never get the best of anything.

Quite a lot was said about teenagers, particularly because they represented a visible and numerically large section of the community. The elder of two brothers spoke about the difficulties of handling them:

> The young ones out there are all hustling—they have their bags, and they like their bags. These little jitterbugs threaten you, and still the parents protect them. The parents protect them even when they're wrong. What else they're going to do?

The concern of these men for the teenagers of the community was not at all surprising. In part it reflected their underlying feeling of failure since their migration. But it also showed their awareness of the problems facing the younger brothers and sisters who represented the future, a future that, if current trends continued, would undoubtedly be much like their own present.

Notwithstanding the deprived conditions they described and the bleak outlook for the teenagers, the men in the study consistently distinguished between structural deprivation and their feelings about the people as Black people. These distinctions are evident in the following comments:

> It's down, the community is good; you have to hustle to survive. It's great, the people, they are good. The other things make it hard.

> Watts is like an economic depression, but the people are graceful, they get along good, although there is a problem all around you and you try to live with it.

Even when contrasted with other, apparently less poverty-ridden Black areas of the city, love of the neighborhood people was still emphasized:

> Watts is a slum. There are some nice houses, but mostly the houses are raggedy and poor, no showers in every house. It's not the type of community I like to live in, although I like the people here better than on the West Side. People are something else, more hypes and dope addicts on the West Side. Now we have winos here; very few heavy users here; on the West Side, they will rip-off from you in a minute. Here the people are good to each other.

This sentiment was so pervasive that often these men found it difficult to speak openly of the existence of Black problems. Some denied any problems; others who did cite them took pains to clarify that Blacks were not solely responsible for the conditions under which they lived or for the way they were dealing with them. This attitude was typified by remarks like this:

> It's a nice place. It's just that some people get hostile; yet it's not a bad place to live in, although it's been called many different names, some good, some not so good. Now there's not too much fighting as before. People are getting an understanding about a whole lot of things.

These men were essentially defending the characteristics of the people. It is the Black response to the condition of racial deprivation that distinguishes the brother or sister embedded in the Black experience from those who attempt to disassociate themselves by denying the impact it has. One youngster explained that, despite the chaos in the streets, he liked living in Watts because: "everybody's themselves. If you talk right, and don't be talking all sadity, things are all right." Others pointed to the sense of community which had developed even in the

midst of suffering. "It's a nice place, because you know everybody and everybody knows you." The importance of people's
ties, of being "down," real, sometimes expressed in other cultures as being of the soil and being ethnically connected, was
great, because Blacks' identity as a group is essential to survival
and to maintaining the sense of community.

Clearly, communal and interpersonal ties were strong.
The young men identified with their community, yet as a group
their future was bleak. The teenagers who sought to realize
a dream found themselves as young adults trapped by events
and social forces that their youthfulness could not affect in any
way. Their housing and family life, which may be used as one
indicator of generational status changes, revealed their fixed im-
mobility. By 1965, none owned his own home. Some complained
of paying very high rents for poor dwellings, but because of the
limited available housing and the high demand they had to accept the situation. The limited area known as Watts in the forties
had expanded by 1965, yet all these men still lived in central
Watts, some in the housing projects, others with extended families. Only a few had married, and of these all except one had
separated. Most had long since terminated school and few had
any salable occupational skills; hence, the majority existed with
severe economic want. Most of their social life took place in and
around the home, since there were still few social centers in the
community.

By 1975, the surface of Watts had changed, but its underlying character remained the same. The many small homes that
once gave it the appearance of being just another small community in sunny Los Angeles were almost gone. The urban renewal
plans implemented in the 1960s had dramatically reshaped the
landscape with rows of similar apartments. Urban renewal had
also changed the location of the former Watts residents. When
the original houses were torn down and replaced by new buildings, many of the former inhabitants were squeezed further
south toward the perimeter of Los Angeles County. This new
area bordering Watts and Compton is densely populated and,
like the old Watts, lacks effective institutions or organizations
through which to generate community power.

Once the area of the Red Car Line in the forties, the main street of small shops in the fifties, and identified in the mid sixties as one of the nation's "charcoal alleys," 103rd Street had by the seventies undergone further change. The rubble was all gone, the streets were lit, and many of the old residents had slowly disappeared. Despite the changes in the landscape that urban renewal had brought, however, the basic conditions of economic stagnation and lack of attention continued. The parking lot was no longer visible, and neither were the men who once occupied that well-known ground. But the conditions that produced social stagnation in 1950 and led to the explosion in 1965 continued, albeit in more subtle forms. The making of the ghetto had been completed.

4

Failure of the Schools

During the fifties and sixties, the magic recipe for success and mobility was education. It was the path the poor and lower class were urged to pursue to achieve upward mobility. For large sections of whites, the educational system had been an effective vehicle to achieve middle-class status. For far too many poor Blacks, it was an abysmal failure.

The educational system presents a fundamental paradox for Blacks. It continues to be held up by the broader society and by Blacks themselves as the institution that makes possible upward mobility, yet Black youths' encounters with it have resulted too often in destroyed aspirations and failure. The community of Blacks criticizes the system for its lack of resources to meet the challenges of ghetto area education. White educators express fear of continued employment in central-city schools as they experience an isolation from and resentment by the ghetto students, yet resist transferring out as they are unwilling to relinquish tenured positions gained from years of service. During the past decade, a large population of whites and some Blacks fled the inner-city enclaves seeking better educational opportunity for their children in suburbia. During that same time the issue of busing polarized Black and white citizens, who poised on the brink of open conflict in response to the Supreme Court's order that all schools "integrate" as a solution to the ever-mounting problem of Black youths' educational failure.

In the mounting debate about the causes of this failure, educators, politicians, and the general public can seemingly agree only that something has gone wrong. Although disagreement continues concerning whether the educational system or the Black student is the core problem, the fact remains that each year a disproportionately large number of inner-city students do not complete their education and the age at which they terminate gets younger and younger. As the severity of this problem became recognized in the sixties, a number of inquiries were begun by legislators and social scientists. One direction of study sought to uncover those factors in the ghetto dwellers' "cultural life," with particular reference to the home environment, that were assumed to affect their absorption of educational material (Birch and Gussow, 1970; Scanzoni, 1971; Wolf, 1965). Other variations on the "culture of poverty" theme, which were discussed in Chapter One, examined environmental factors with special relevance to the inhabitants' control, use of power, and participation as variables affecting educational attainment (Dervin and Greenberg, 1972; Kimbrough, 1964). Further studies were undertaken on curriculum content and organization, for example, Dickeman (1973), Fantini and Weinstein (1968), Gordon (1968–1969), and Taba and Elkins (1966). There were other studies on the educability of ghetto youth, such as Zigler (1966). Some focused on their learning styles (Leichter, 1973), while others searched for disjunctive factors in ethnic living patterns that could account for the differences in educational achievement of Blacks and whites. The Supreme Court's decision supporting desegregation of education heavily influenced the issues and direction of this research (Coleman, 1966; Gordon, 1968–1969; U.S. Commission on Civil Rights, 1976). Some studies examined whether ghetto youths' widespread use of "Black language," as opposed to mainstream "school language," affected their learning abilities (Cordesco, 1973; Horner, 1966). In the end, even the structural components of the school environment were examined with special concern for its effect on education (Friedman, 1962; Raskin, 1968).

Much of this research had an underlying premise that being Black (and poor) was directly related to educational underachievement. Because educators and legislators, whether consciously or unconsciously, believed this premise was fact, they developed and supported numerous programs that sought to supplement and compensate for what was assumed to be either missing or insufficient ingredients in the ghetto youths' life. Thus, programs geared to cultural enrichment and deficit compensation gained attention. Reports regarding the effectiveness of these efforts vary. Some claim good results, others admit only limited or no success. Notwithstanding some dubious findings, these studies did contribute to our understanding of some learning dynamics of poverty populations. But despite the reform efforts occasioned by the research, the number of poor Black males being dumped early in the educational journey continued to mount steadily.

The subjects of this study were typical young dropouts. Between the ages of fourteen and seventeen, all but six of the thirty left school (the majority in the twelfth grade). Either they quit or they were expelled because of "disruptive and antisocial behavior," "argumentativeness," aggressive confrontation of instructors, and truancy. For five of the six who did graduate, high school represented the end of their formal education; the sixth attended junior college for a semester before discontinuing. This was a tragic result in view of the hopes they had when they arrived in Watts.

Aspirations and Alienation

Only a few years earlier these young men had looked forward to attending city schools and leaving the small schools of their southern communities. In retrospect, they realized how much they had liked their old schools, despite the obvious limitations of both space and materials. The common ethnicity of the pupils and teachers, the familiarity of the educational referents, the deep peer associations in and out of school had made it a community experience. Most of all, there was a feeling that the teachers cared, that "they forced the best out of us," as one student said. Still, at the time of the migration they had thought urban schools might offer more. So without knowing what was in store for them in Watts, they entered school with both nervous anticipation and hopeful expectation. School was seen as the key to the future, to a good JOB, and they wanted to do well. Most aspired to graduate from high school at least. Such achievement would have fulfilled the hopes of their parents, too, whose daily preachment was "Stay in school and get that high school diploma." Six members of the study group had even higher ambitions, believing that possessing a college degree would enable them to "make it in a big way."

Thus, contrary to popular belief, these ghetto men did have educational aspirations. The trouble was that their goals were vague and lacked specificity. Their educational pursuits were encouraged by the message of their parents and the broader society. Since they had been taught that securing a job and obtaining those commodities deemed valuable by society required finishing school, they sought to do this. For most of these men, education was not something intrinsically valuable; it was strictly a utilitarian means to a good job, money, and therefore status. This in itself was not as problematic as the fact that they had no clear understanding of how to use education to gain career objectives—of which groups of courses would lead to which vocations. Therefore, although their early educational aspirations were important, they were not a reliable predictor of achievement, since aspirations without proper nurturing can easily fail.

The responsibility for the gap between aspirations and success must be laid primarily at the educational doorstep. The school system of Watts did not meet the needs of these young people in a variety of ways. To put the issue most broadly, the system mishandled its socialization function. Educators would agree that a basic purpose of schooling is to teach students how to be a successful part of the culture. It should give them the knowledge and skills they need to deal with the social environment, help them find out what roles are available to them, what society expects of them, and how they might attain the legitimate goals that society offers. By studying the learning materials and observing effective models, the student should understand the history, mores, values, and beliefs of his society. Unfortunately, however, the Watts' schools failed to perform this function, in the main, because they tried to make the Black students adapt only to the mainstream society and excluded the positive relevancies of the Black students' environments.

These young ghetto dwellers entered school with expectations that did not differ significantly from most American youngsters. But shortly after they started high school, the fundamental differences between their expectations and orientations and those of the school system became more openly recognized and eventually led to real conflict. According to the men in the study, the teachers and the educational materials had expected them to adopt paths to success and forms of behavior with which they were largely unfamiliar and which had little association with their daily lives. "It was as if everything being taught was new, strange, and didn't seem to have any use." Most of the stories they read and the examples given in the books or by the teachers were about another society, the white world. To them, mainstream society was different, if not unnatural. In attempting to explain this feeling, without any special anger, one man said, "We don't live there; we don't live like that, and, man, they are just different."

The Black world, in which the Watts men grew and developed and to which they were deeply attached, included their brothers and sisters, cousins and aunts, even the jobless and people on welfare and some hurting folks—all of whom were seen as natural members of the community. Side by side with this existed the people who went to work, to church, those who sang Black songs, and those who listened to James Brown. Black life did not have to be chitterlings, greens, or chops; and Black people did not all have to sit around the table at dinner time. But for the young men, music and rhythm were functional parts of life, along with being poor and having to deal with harassment. In essence, Black life had a different pace, style, and requirements for survival. These were the elements felt to be totally absent from the school experience and the class materials. As one man put it:

> I am not jiving, but they don't tell you how to duck the police and keep from being jacked up. They never

taught me how to live on three dollars a week. They never even told me about the Supremes; instead, you know what this music teacher was trying to get us to listen to? Some long-haired dude, some foreigner.

The proselytizing of a strange model of life, by both white teachers and integrationist Black instructors, engendered some discomfort and alienation. However, what really made these men angry was the explicit and implicit put-down of those things that were the core of their lives. For example, Black dance, music, and modes of communication were viewed negatively and characterized as improper. Additionally, their whole living environment—their parents and community people in general; 103rd Street and the other ghetto streets with the mom-and-pop stores, small Black-owned shops, and hangouts; their homes, furnishings, food, and social codes—was assigned a negative value or at best not given appropriate respect.

The message of cultural inferiority was conveyed in myriad ways, from outright speech corrections to the omission of everyday Black referents and the absence of Black history in the curriculum. Their African heritage and the story of Blacks' impact on this country were largely ignored; in fact, many of these men were left with the distinct impression that their history began with grandmother and grandfather chopping cotton in the southern fields. One member of the study group reflected on the covert humiliation: "I don't need the man [the teacher] to tell me directly that my way of life is uncivilized, but I know what he's putting down; I ain't nobody's fool."

Understandably, the young ghetto Blacks reacted to this treatment with resentment and defensiveness. From their standpoint, the community of Blacks was not an essentially negative environment, for all its hardship and suffering. And what major negative qualities it had were not considered the fault of the inhabitants but the consequences of mainstream's having closed out opportunity and confined them. Compounding their antagonistic feelings was the fact that the schools were trying to engage them in an almost impossible adaptation at the same time they were undergoing the intense identity search of adolescence. At this age the socializing function of the streets, of peer culture, supersedes all other efforts to mold social skills, including even those of the family. The pressure to identify with Black life, not to reject it, was never greater. To develop personal identity and maintain integrity, they had to become part of their milieu. In this world there were natural forms of Black communication and social customs that dictated their relations to each other. There were the idols of the community, the sports figures, the important Reverend; there were the foods, the flavor, and special smells; there were Black women. And there were the traditions of social display, the dress styles, the mannerisms—all the things one must know to be "in," to "get down and know what's happening." (See Erikson, 1966, for further discussion.)

In short, the Watts school system pushed an alien orientation while the young ghetto residents tried with great intensity to master their real and current environment. They did not believe their world was an anomaly or a transient social phenomenon. They did not think they would depart from Watts to a new middle-class life on the other part of town. Thus, the institution of education and its agents, the administrators and teachers, were experienced as antagonistic elements in these youths' socialization rather than as facilitators of their goals.

In addition to this cultural-ideological conflict, there existed also the demonstrated inability of the schools to move young Blacks effectively into the opportunity system. Misdirected and poor counseling were part of this problem. The high schools seldom helped the Black students transform their early aspirations by pointing out the range of vocations available and making clear the need to take particular courses in order to attain a specific career goal. They also failed to encourage students to seek careers that required a higher education, as mentioned in the last chapter; neither did they help the ghetto students refine their objectives and redirect their efforts accordingly.

Possibly even more important, they neglected to openly point out those areas that were not available because of racism. Although the schools' attempts to get these students to adopt mainstream behavior and values implied a promise to provide access to the world of success, the school system was totally ineffective at doing so. The men cited many examples of people they knew who had finished high school, yet were unable to get jobs because of job market discrimination. The job-hunting experiences of the men, particularly those who had participated in training and rehabilitation programs, further confirmed the belief that Blacks are not provided unimpeded access to mainstream opportunity, even if they go along with the educational socializing process. As one eighteen-year-old noted:

> Even if you had training and know how to do the job, once you show up and ask for the machine operating job, and the man sees you, he wants to give you a broom and start you sweeping. Well, I'd rather not work than sweep no floor.

The skepticism and hardened attitudes resulting from these experiences reinforced their resistance to absorbing the schools' perspective. Thus, the whole system of education was seen as encouraging the ghetto youth to seek goals that were unattainable, not because of individual incapacity but because of the widespread effect of racism, which shrinks employment opportunities, increases the competition among Blacks, and furthers the disconnection between the educational system and the job world.

Attitudes Toward Multiracial Schooling

Most of the men in the study group had experienced both segregated schools and predominantly white or racially mixed schools. More than 85 percent went to all-Black schools in the South before they migrated. During the early years in Watts, the schools contained about equal proportions of whites, Mexican-Americans, and Blacks. But this period of balance was short-lived, as we saw in Chapter Two, and by the late fifties they found themselves in segregated schools again. Given this background, it was inevitable that the issue of "integrated" schools would come up whenever education was discussed. With some reservations, over 80 percent of the men expressed a preference for integrated education. They felt that a racially mixed school, since it was generally geared to white achievement, would offer better facilities, more committed teachers, and more learning materials. They also felt they would receive more encouragement, directly and indirectly, to continue their education and would therefore be more motivated. A typical expression of this sentiment was voiced by one of the older men who had attended school in Watts while the composition of the student body changed:

> When they [Black children] go to school with mixed classes, where there are mostly whites, they get a higher IQ. The teachers and powers bring out the best. [In contrast] on 102nd Street, the schools do not instill enough discipline. The teachers give up too fast.

Even while acknowledging these benefits of biracial schooling, the men differed with the social scientists and educators who express concern about the "culture of poverty" and question the "educability" of ghetto youth and see "integrated education" as a remedial solution to the problem of Black underachievement. These men did not believe, as do many social researchers, that simply attending schools with whites directly contributes to more effective absorption of the educational material. They believed that the difference, if it does occur, is due more to the teachers' commitment, attitudes, expectations, and consequent demands. Of course, teacher commitment does affect classroom atmosphere and influence student behavior; in turn, peer behavior affects individual readiness to learn. But what concerned these men was correcting the inference that they could not do well without whites. Their concern was also a reaction to their feeling that in integrated education they are the residual and not the primary focus of educators.

A very perceptive minority of the study group expressed preference for an all-Black educational system. In contrasting their experiences in the South with those in the racially mixed schools of Watts, they maintained that integrated education more often had a negative effect on their learning and personal development. Schools dominated by whites stressed an Anglo-oriented curriculum and neglected or more often "put-down" ethnic groups' contributions, which they felt created an experience of negative difference:

> I want them [young Blacks] to grow up around their own people, because if they grow up with mostly white, the colored feel less important than whites.

All the men expressed a similar poignant concern for the future education of Black children, but in view of the current school conditions, particularly exemplified by the large numbers of school-age youth in the streets, most were not prepared to argue strongly for all-Black schooling. What they opted for instead was integrated schools in which the majority of students were Black:

> Surely, not mostly white, because the kids would feel inferior. If more whites are there, they gain the advantage and always get the positions when they become available. And the Black kids wouldn't understand this till later, and by then feel bad.

Thus, the majority of the men generally supported the federal push for integrated education, yet with mixed feelings. They had positive memories of belonging in southern all-Black schools. Despite the material inadequacies of those institutions, the teachers showed concern, taught them appropriate Black customs, provided real and consistent models to emulate, and most of all were socially available. Despite the reality of second-class status held in broader southern life, they were educated in Black schools with first-class respect because they were to become the future leaders of Blacks. But all-Black education in Watts, with its emphasis on negative difference and unnatural separation, was worse than segregated education in the South. In the end, the assessed advantages of biracial education outweighed their reservations, although they clearly felt that those advantages could be rendered negligible if Black students were in the minority—and therefore would receive less attention and opportunity. The option finally favored by most of the men was for integrated but Black-dominated schooling, a clearly different distribution of students than is traditionally perceived. To effect this, it would require that white students, and presumably faculty, be redistributed to predominantly Black schools in ratios that increased their presence but did not alter the dominance of Blacks.

Alternative Striving Adaptations

Clearly, education presents a series of dilemmas for the young inner-city Black. There are basically three alternative ways to respond. First, he may choose to adopt the perspective of the educational system. This requires that he reject the ghetto elements—its customs and beliefs, its resistive spirit, and even his peers—in his self-development activity. This choice further requires, despite the lack of supportive evidence, that he alienate himself from his immediate social base and believe that a viable alternative opportunity system and social context awaits him if he accomplishes the transformation.

The second option is to make a somewhat marginal adaptation. He selects those behaviors from both Black and non-Black life that he considers socially positive and individually enhancing. This adjustment then means relinquishing some indigenous practices while integrating selected "alien" cultural values, social patterns, and perspectives. This process approximates the bicultural or integration model.

Third, he may adopt as the locus of his aspirations the Black milieu, the social context that has the most familiarity, comfort, and connectedness. Although seemingly the most consistent and logical environment, nevertheless, this choice poses the most severe consequences. Since achievement that is confined to the Black context is judged less desirable than mainstream success, both by whites and some Blacks, he must be ready to accept "second-class" status even if he "makes it" in the Black world. The persistence of lower economic ceilings in the Black community (discussed in Chapter Five) also affects the level of real achievement possible.

These young men considered the first adaptation the least feasible, because in spite of the ambivalent wishes they did not perceive middle-class America as a truly attainable social context. They saw it as a separate, segregated, and closed system, though they knew some Blacks who functioned in it. They were also aware that even the Black person who gained middle-class status was not really much more than just another Black man facing socially imposed constraints on his opportunities and levels of achievements. Possibly the greatest resistence to adopting this mode of striving was the necessary rejection of his natural background and spiritual separation from his inherited community.

The second alternative was also rejected by most the men, albeit with great reservations and conflict. Adopting this eclectic model of striving required not only incorporating values from two different cultures (becoming culturally pluralistic)—which meant rejecting much of their cultural heritage as negative while incorporating a cultural mode that was presented as if it were faultless. Such a process encourages young Blacks to dissociate themselves from their history of slavery—more directly, the slave, the person and family member—and to find a present and future with the American mobility dream and with those who have acculturated and attained mainstream acheivement. This choice was seen by these men as the one made by many middle-class Black achievers of the fifties and sixties. Despite a desire for the incomes and commodities of middle-classness, they consciously resisted becoming alienated from what they perceived to be their relevant Black life. Their resistance was greatly supported by the many new positive Black community developments, spirit, and images that emerged for emulation in the late sixties.

The rejection of the second model by these young men presents a significant problem for future strivers; it points to one source of the conflict between lower-class and middle-class Blacks in the sixties and heightens awareness of the importance of a solid home and community base in attempts to achieve. For in 1965, the majority of these ghetto-bound men felt estranged from middle-class Blacks, in part because they perceived them as spending an inordinate amount of energy and time getting away from Black association. The middle-class strivers were seen as having adopted white attitudes, thinking modes, and actions and as deemphasizing their Black identity and community connectedness. This estrangement was strengthened by the fact that upwardly mobile Blacks regularly disappeared from the central-city social life as soon as they had achieved. And lastly, the activity generated by Black community leaders in the sixties provided these men with hope that a functionally viable Black community was emerging—one that would make mobility within a Black context appear to be more than a dream.*

The third choice, adaptation within the Black community context was seen by these young men as the most logical and natural course. They preferred to strive in familiar surroundings, among family and friends, and in an environment that was not alien. But as indicated earlier, this decision almost automatically presages failure, because it brings them into conflict with the value base of the educational system, which is attempting to "acculturate" them or get them to adopt mainstream values and objectives. Those the schools are unable to convert are dubbed failures, even though much of the conflict is due to the system's inability to provide palatable alternatives to the isolationism of the ghetto youth. Such labeling as "dropout" or

---

*Variations in mobility striving patterns by Blacks deserve much more study, particularly the Black communities of Atlanta and Washington, D.C., in the late thirties and forties. Blacks raised in these small and tightly knit societies strove for high-level functional roles within the opportunity systems of Black society, primarily in a Black political and economic life. Although they tended to adopt artifacts, social customs, and behavioral styles of upper-class white life, they probably experienced a lesser feeling of alienation or marginality than did the middle-class strivers of the fifties and sixties, as the goals and indicators of success were located in the Black community and principally involved searching for social and economic roles with Black people. (For greater discussion of Black behavioral style adaptations see Dollard, 1949; Frazier, 1956; and Hare, 1965.) When Blacks sought upward mobility in mainstream society, they sought social and economic roles where the Black strivers had lower status and were disfavored competitors. Attainment of unequal status may not be the only cause of the stress associated with achievement-oriented Blacks; this stress may have much to do with their having to meet the tasks (very often inhumane) which were set as a condition of passage to abridged achievement.

"educational failure" indelibly marks the victim as ineligible for future passage through other institutions. Thus inner-city youth, such as these men, who decide to maintain their identification with central-city Black life, also increase their chances of being rejected. Paradoxically, this choice more often derives from personal survival instincts than from any clearly thought out examination of the consequences of taking this path.

From teachers' comments, public reports, and other sources, the young men in the study group received various conflicting explanations for their failure; understandably, they developed great ambivalence on the subject. On the one hand, they sometimes acknowledged the possibility that they lacked capacity and perhaps could not grasp and apply the required bodies of knowledge. One of the manifestations of this doubt was self-depreciation regarding natural intelligence. Hence, some assumed the onus of failure:

> Man, I wasn't the smartest dude, you know, I just didn't dig that book and reading stuff too much. I think I could have made it, but some of that stuff was too much, I just didn't understand it. Now, I am much better at mechanical things.

Possibly the most tragic were those who accepted their failure as stemming from their personal inadequacies when, in fact, it had been systemically engendered. And in the case of many of these men, negative self-assessment was challenged by their extremely clever and most intelligent problem-solving abilities. Day-to-day experience with them showed that the raw ability was there, only the formal learning was absent. However, because they had been expelled or had quit school, many had internalized the negative characterization "dropout" and had begun to accept themselves as being less than adequate. Thus the cycle—failure in the schools, the defensive turn-off of formal learning situations, more failure—was reinforced.

Assuming an anti-intellectual posture is another way in which ghetto youth react to mainstream education's rejection of their life situation and culture. In the face of being denied

positive referents and use of their life experience, and con-
trastingly receiving a continuous bombardment of mainstream
ways, these men close their minds, consciously warding off absorbing the material or setting up psychological blocks against
receiving mainstream-oriented materials. These behaviors are
rewarded by peers who exert pressure to discourage them from
showing interest in school or in those things assumed to be connected to mainstream cultural life. It sometimes becomes almost
taboo for the young aspirant to admit to having any interest in
attending or participating in broader community activities.

A somewhat different response, representing the other
side of the coin, which supports an anti-mainstream intellectual
stance is the youths' exclusive use of Black vernacular and Black
referents. Through the concentrated and sole use of a Black
mode, they express and articulate a view of events from their
perception—and it is a reaction to mainstream dominance. In
the end, the vernacular is theirs, the referents are theirs, the
perspective is theirs—and Black.

Yet, such survival devices do not erase the fact that failure produces immobility and with it a great sense of helplessness. In this tragic situation the men felt deeply the absence of
support, particularly from those they thought could potentially
bring some relief—Black educators and other community achievers. Starkly absent from their lives were the real Black success
models. When most of these young men transferred from southern rural schools to urban ghetto schools, they expected to see
many more Blacks in important walks of life, including teaching,
and expected to have access to them as they did in their pre-
migratory homes. But they found only a few Black teachers,
and these seemed to be under exceptional pressure from their
white colleagues to show not only that they were different from
newly arrived and poorer Blacks but also that they felt no special kinship with them as Blacks.

The resultant estrangement compounded the Black students' sense of isolation and their rejection of school. They felt
distant from and unable to relate to those who composed the
educational system. To neutralize these feelings, they very
much needed personal contact with their teachers, but they

seldom had it in the formal relationships encountered in Watts classrooms or in the informal social life of the community. Educators have placed great stress on discipline and structured control in ghetto schools, believing that ghetto youngsters are unable to use freedom or innovative classroom experiences. Yet instead of creating a better learning environment, as they were presumably trying to do, these educators have made learning more difficult for the ghetto students, who equated structured control with distance, and thus provided one more rejection in an otherwise culturally dissonant experience. The separation between the Black students and their white teachers was generally accepted as natural. The white educator presented no dilemma, as he was viewed as "alien" and thus any extended social ties outside the classroom would be considered exceptional and special. What disturbed the students much more was their separation from the Black educators who they perceived as their natural allies in a difficult environment. As expressed by one young man, "they [the Black teachers] were so uptight about being right, they didn't have no time for us, so we just used to say fuck them, and go on about our business."

The accumulated negative experiences that ghetto youths receive in their educational journey lead them to develop harsh views of educators, the system, and its function in the community. Although only a minority had this opinion at first, the men later held that ghetto education is actually intended to demoralize Blacks and assure that they do not make it. In other words, many now believe that the educational system does not really fail in its function but rather fulfills its covert purpose: to perpetuate a permanent underachieving, socially obsolete group of Blacks. This view was expressed rather heatedly as follows:

> Any organization, be it education or otherwise, that produces as many rejects and dropouts as ghetto schools, it would have been scrapped long ago. The man don't keep no inefficient business. He's too smart for that.

But whether one believes that the educational failure of ghetto youth is due to purposeful rejection by the schools, to an unintended malfunctioning of the system, to the difficulty of resolving the conflict between ghetto life and mainstream life, or even to individual incapacity, the fact remains—they are failing in record numbers. Unfortunately, when Blacks depart the educational system they are unaware of the full impact of what has happened. Only when they encounter closed doors to employment opportunity, especially to the better jobs requiring some skill and offering steady incomes, does the reality of being a "dropout," a system reject, come into focus dramatically.

Once young Blacks leave school—and the earlier that happens, the worse off they are—they usually lose access both to further schooling and to the job market. For a variety of reasons, including peer pressure, the poor self-image resulting from the dropout label, and a reluctance to renounce the ghetto culture context and endure further humiliation and failure, the terminators do not go back to school after quitting or being rejected. Of the men in the study group, only three reentered formal educational institutions. Six others did receive some vocational training in jail (one of the most common sources of obtaining job skills for ghetto youth), and some of the men obtained special training from the Office of Economic Opportunity programs offered in Watts after the 1965 rebellion. In the main, however, any skills they managed to acquire after leaving school were developed on the job. And in most cases only menial jobs or no jobs were open to them.

In the final analysis, the ghetto educational system has, whether or not consciously, immobilized ghetto youth, creating a technically obsolete class. Because the educational structure of Watts was unable to socialize ghetto students for new roles in society, did not provide clear connections between schooling and the job world, and remained ineffective at enhancing the advancement of these Black youths, it in fact contributed significantly to their early obsolescence and their entrance into the underclass.

5

Chronic
Unemployment

At this point, we have a vivid picture of the pool of unused man-power that is collecting in ghettos across the country. It is com-posed primarily of young men (younger than the mass of Black unemployed of earlier decades) who have no educational cre-dentials, who have had very little vocational training and lack the technological skills demanded by a sophisticated and swiftly changing job market, who consequently are destitute (estimated annual income $1,200 to $2,000), and who, above all, must contend with racism every day of their lives. The combination of these characteristics results in this group of Blacks becoming fixed at the bottom of the economic ladder, able to obtain only cellar-level jobs that are often seasonal or part-time. Their im-mobility is not primarily due to personal disabilities—most are healthy, energetic, intelligent, and uniquely creative in the ways of survival—but to that morass of social conditions which even-tually defies any one individual's effort to neutralize it.

To begin to break the cycle of entrapment, these under-class men must have steady work, for employment not only pro-vides money and its accompaniments—the chance to obtain credit, to buy property, to make investments—but has much to do with building one's sense of self-worth. Thus "I need a JOB, a J-O-B is where it's at" is their constant cry. Welfare or hustling may suffice when there is no other way, but they are no substitute for regular, adequately paid work.

Responses of Other Segments of Society

How have other people reacted to the condition of the underclass, to the demands for work? Among Blacks of other classes, the existence of this population and its often destructive effects on Black community life have become cause for alarm and concern. In recognition of this problem, Black institutions such as the Urban League have urged the federal government to create massive employment programs. Black legislators have sought to reorganize social welfare provisions to make a broader impact on this population by providing jobs instead of maintenance payments. Others have tried through congressional legislation (H.R. 50) to make full employment a national goal. And various Black business ventures have been initiated with a view to employing some small numbers of this group. But so far, at least, none of these efforts has stemmed the tide of underclass unemployment.

Mainstream social analysts are aware of this significant development, but they have chosen to respond circuitously. Currently its members emphasize the emerging Black middle class, citing figures on Black success and mobility. Their reports are used to confirm the myth that Black mobility parallels that of white, while drawing attention away from the persistent, deep-seated problem of the growing underclass. They tend to convey the false notion that middle-class attainment, and therefore unencumbered access to mainstream opportunity, is typical of the majority of Blacks. But, in fact, this is not so (Williams, 1979; McAdoo, Harriette, and Pipes, 1979). A similar impression is given by reports on the entrepreneurial gains of Blacks. These purport to show that many new small business achievements, particularly those supported by federal funds, represent significant progress by former low-income Blacks.

An earlier and somewhat promising approach by the social science community had been to recognize the problem existing in the socioeconomic inequality of Blacks and whites. This recognition was most prominent in reports that uncovered pockets of poverty among specific unique populations in America, particularly Blacks (Harrington, 1966). However, these pockets, it was said, were created by long-term societal racism and thereby contributed to deficits in the development of Blacks' psychological character. It was even further emphasized that racism (identified in its "institutional" form) also contributed to the exclusion of Blacks from economic opportunity in the broader society (Kerner, 1968). An entirely new nomenclature was developed to describe this condition. We heard not only about the "disadvantaged" and the "culturally deprived" but about "deficit character," "thwarted characterological development" (most often hypothesized as stemming from years of deprivation), and the "culture of poverty." Instead of directing major effort to opening up economic opportunity—to jobs, new careers, union membership, on-the-job training, and upgrading programs—social planners suggested an emphasis on psychosocial rehabilitative programs (Donovan, 1967). These were supposed to reverse the experience of cultural deprivation and thus allow poor Blacks to more adequately manipulate and participate in their surroundings. The underlying assumption of this approach was that racism was not as important a deterrent to Black progress as were the personal inadequacies with which Blacks were saddled. This assumption also implicitly supported the notion that the free enterprise system was an open market and that failure to enter it or to fully exploit it was due to personal inability, not market constraints.

And so what began as a promising, balanced analysis became focused only on individual defects; the role of racism was largely ignored. Thus the strategy evolved to hold ghetto individuals themselves responsible for their underachievement. The policy was to seek reasons for ghettoization (once again) in the individual rather than in the systems that produced the condition. By focusing on individual Black underachievement, this approach rationalized an economic organization based on discrimination.

Hence, as prompted by the social scientists' proposals, the federal government's response to a rising, and increasingly visible, underclass has been inconsistent and ineffective. Lyndon Johnson's War on Poverty programs were intended to acculturate poor Blacks, in line with the social analysts' emphasis on undoing the effects of cultural deprivation, and to train them to meet the occupational challenges of the Great Society. The latter programs, which included giving federal support to private industry to train and absorb some of the untrained-unemployed poor, had only a limited impact, however. Part of the problem was that private business did not become very involved, and the government training efforts were directed at such low-level jobs that even if the trainees had been able to get these jobs they would not have obtained adequate incomes or jobs with career lines. But basically the trouble was the same as always: These programs did not come to grips with the discriminatory practices that barred poor Blacks from equal employment opportunity, and therefore they were unable to move large numbers from poverty and underclass stagnation to the status of income-earning, productive citizens. Although the Civil Rights Act of 1964, and the affirmative action programs that flowed from it, was a sweeping attempt to prevent discrimination against minorities and to bring about fair employment practices, among other things, its implementation has been troubled and sketchy. The affirmative action thrust has provided some upward movement for a limited number, but it certainly has not enabled large numbers of inner-city Blacks to obtain steady work, much less to enter upwardly mobile paths. And in the past few years affirmative action programs increasingly being referred to as "reverse discrimination," have foundered on the shoals of recession, white backlash, and ineffective enforcement.

The Nixon and Ford administrations generally withdrew support from these broad social programs, although a highly touted "Black capitalism" scheme, designed to revitalize the Black community by offering low-interest loans to aspiring Black business people, was launched. Examination of this plan discloses, however, that it was not aimed at employing significant numbers of the underclass. Some reformers during this period encouraged the poor to develop skills in "community change" and to "participate" as a way of altering ghetto life; this proposal seems positive until we see it as another way for the mainstream to sidestep its duty to employ the manpower being wasted in dark ghettos. In the end, then, despite some recognition of the role played by institutional racism in perpetuating the underclass and some attempts to remedy the situation, the poor remained as trapped as ever while the myth was perpetuated that they were individually responsible for their condition as well as for curing it.

Aspirations and Achievement

The basis for the mainstream opinion about the underclass, as noted earlier, was the contention that ghetto youth have only limited aspirations, are poorly motivated to strive for betterment (preferring "handouts"), and do not invest the energy necessary for success in a competitive job market. In other words, we have here an aspect of the "personal inadequacy" explanation for their failure. Without question, differences in the makeup, experience, and capacity of individual Blacks have had, and will continue to have, an important influence on the variations seen in Black levels of achievement. However, social scientists have hidden behind the body of knowledge on individual differences, avoiding a balanced examination of the causes of underachievement. Consequently, few studies of the work aspirations and attitudes of young underclass males have been undertaken, and the stereotypes persist. This study of the young men of Watts therefore sought in particular to find out more about what kinds of jobs they desired, what limited their aspirations and achievements, and so on.

Worlds of Aspiration. Because racism is an institutionalized part of American life, two worlds always exist for Blacks—the Black community and parts of the mainstream. To the degree that they are available as alternatives, Blacks must decide in which world they seek to achieve. This factor affected the work aspirations of the Watts men no less than those of others. In their case, there was even a third possibility created by the division of the Black world into legitimate and illegitimate economic systems. The former consists of small businesses—including the Black media, the mom-and-pop stores, the barber shops and beauty parlors—that have traditionally catered to Black tastes and interests and provided those commodities that are unique to Black life and traditions. (Some of these goods are nearly impossible to obtain elsewhere.) This economic system, which clearly depends on the existence of an indigenous Black population separated from the mainstream, in many ways parallels that of the broader society but on a smaller scale and with a decidedly lower economic ceiling.

Social scientists have recognized the existence of parallel sociocultural systems, describing elaborate Black subcultures or life-styles and pointing out how Blacks use mainstream systems in one way and their own in quite a different manner. But they have paid little attention to the parallel economic structures, and especially to the effect the Black economic network has on the aspirations of underclass youth. Instead, the social analysts have focused on the illegitimate livelihoods—hustling, prostitution, gambling, drug trafficking—purporting to show that these are the primary sources of income for ghettoized poor Blacks. Although these activities certainly exist (and are examined in a later chapter), there is serious question whether they are controlled by Blacks or whether they do indeed provide incomes for large numbers of Blacks—significant factors in ghetto economics.

The importance of the legitimate system as an alternative for those youths who do not seek entry into the mainstream and who do not want to be involved in criminal enterprises is suggested by the fact that more than 15 percent of the study men aspired to jobs in this context. Several even wanted to own or manage a small business. Such aspirations cannot be considered low. Though the monetary returns would be somewhat less than those of comparable mainstream enterprises, because of the lower ceilings characteristic of the Black economic sector, the status accorded would be equal if not sometimes higher. Besides steady and relatively high incomes and status, these vocations offer two other incentives to the aspirant. First, they are more accessible, in that the Black system sets up no racial barriers; and second, they allow the job holder to function wholly within Black life, a not inconsiderable benefit, since striving in the mainstream often produces psychological stress and failure.

Despite the existence of this indigenous source of jobs and income, however, 80 percent of the men in the study aspired to work in the broader society, in part because there are simply fewer jobs available in Black enterprises. Most of the occupations sought in the mainstream were clustered on the lower-middle range, in terms of the "occupational prestige scale" that ranks ninety occupations (Hodge, Siegel, and Rossi, 1966). The highest-ranked job classifications selected by the men were "machinists" and "social worker" (both listed at 45); next came "manager of small store" (49), "carpenter" (58), "garage mechanic" (62), "machine operator" (64.5), "filling station attendant" (74.5), and "janitor" (85.5). "Shoe shiner," which represents the bottom of the scale at 90, was not selected by any of the respondents in the study group. The majority made selections in the 45–64.5 range, which could be expected to provide yearly incomes in the $9,000–$11,000 bracket. Although none of the men aspired to be doctors, lawyers, physicists, or other upper-income persons, the selection they made still represented high aspirations in relation to their present condition and experience. In 1967, for example, their average weekly earnings were $43 a week, or $2,315 a year. Furthermore, as indicated earlier, most of these men had experienced only seasonal, part-time, and short-term employment. Most held jobs from one to eight months a year. Some had worked only two days a week during their employment periods; others had had continuous work for six to nine weeks. Typically, they worked as floor sweepers, butlers, porters, shoe shiners, janitors, trash removers, and car washers—in other words, in menial, low-level, manual jobs. A small number had had experience in a somewhat higher category of unskilled employment, which still required no specialized education. Included here were jobs as laundry pullers, grinders in foundaries, flat-tire repairers, hod carriers,

and building construction helpers. Some of the men boasted of
having been machine operators, but closer examination disclosed that they had actually been helpers or had had one or
more opportunities to operate a machine in the absence of, or
in relief of, the regular operator. Since these were all nonunion
jobs and sometimes controlled by seasonal factors that dictated
periods of high productivity (speed-up work) and long periods
of lay-off, the men never had assurance of being recalled to
work when the job ended. In short, they had experienced only
unemployment or underemployment.

   Job Characteristics Influencing Aspirations. For the preceding reasons, these men looked for certain qualities in the
jobs they aspired to. First, of course, did the job offer *steady*
work and a reasonable wage? Second, did it provide opportunities for advancement and training? Much time was spent trying
to find paths to a job that would not be a dead end. Third, was
the occupation realistically attainable, that is, not closed by
racism—as evidenced by the presence of Blacks already employed? Fourth, did it have some prestige, particularly within
the Black community? It is important to realize, in relation to
the level of status to which the men aspired, that whites and
Blacks do not accord the same status to certain occupations.
For example, the athlete has been an important person and
model of success for Black youth for a long time. A man like
Muhammed Ali not only symbolizes what can be done with
talent and ability but shows that the "man" and his system can
be beat. So for the Watts men, aspiring to be a professional
athlete or coach represents a high goal, in terms of prestige,
whereas in the broader society in the past such jobs had a lower
status, principally because they did not require an advanced
education. Another role that has somewhat more prestige among
Blacks is that of the educator. The grade school teacher, for example, although traditionally viewed in the mainstream as making an important professional contribution, is increasingly considered the provider of the second income in a middle-class
family. For Blacks, elementary school teaching is a more socially important job and often provides the primary family
income. These differences in status are due, once again, to ra-

cism, which shrinks the opportunities available, even among middle-class Blacks. Those occupations to which Blacks can gain entry therefore obtain a higher status if they provide an important social function and a steady income.

The final characteristic that affected the men's aspirations was the amount of formal learning the job required. Understandably, some of the men desired occupations in which success depends on native ability and skill rather than education. The jobs of athlete, artist, and musician obviously meet this criterion.

It's clear, then, that the views of the public, as well as of social scientists, concerning the underclass's lack of aspirations or low aspirations are inaccurate. Generally speaking, the occupational desires of the young Watts rebels approximated those of mainstream youth. However, it is also apparent that the nature of their aspirations, their motivation to strive for their goals, and their ability to achieve their aims were restricted.

Limiting Factors. Lack of knowledge about the magnitude of vocational possibilities was one limitation. Most of these men had been exposed only to a very narrow portion of the job world. Just about everyone they knew was not working or had the same kinds of low-level jobs they had. The classic underemployment of Blacks within the full spectrum of mainstream occupational roles inevitably means that ghetto youth do not see other Blacks successfully performing a wide variety of roles. And therefore they also lack both formal and casual contacts with capable models—contacts that are so important for gaining information about different jobs, appropriate work behavior, and expectations. In addition, as was noted in Chapter Four, the high schools have seldom helped Blacks understand specific occupations or encouraged them to pursue a career more purposefully. Almost two thirds of the study men spoke of being confused and ill informed regarding particular jobs and the skills needed to obtain them.

In the absence of other sources, the men learned whatever they did know via the informal, word of mouth system of street communication. Although almost 90 percent of them said this system had increased their knowledge of potential job areas —many had started with very limited and fuzzy ideas about occupational choices, having arrived in Watts with the generalized mind set that all they wanted was a J-O-B, any job—this mode of communication had obvious drawbacks. It did offer some guidance on how to apply oneself and act in order to secure specific jobs, particularly those unskilled jobs for which no standardized qualifications are used to determine who is hired, but it directed the men primarily toward those positions in which Blacks had previously succeeded.

As a result, these men knew little about, and gave scant attention to, jobs that racial discrimination had closed to Blacks. More than 95 percent did not attempt to break open new areas or risk failure or delayed achievement by pursuing a "potential" occupation.

When we analyze these various factors limiting the men's aspirations, we see that they are once more largely the result of racism in the form of systems barriers. Hence, for the young Black male, a large part of his thoughts about what he might like to do, and all actions taken in that direction, are influenced by mainstream society's discriminatory practices.

Although at first it is generally difficult to comprehend the subtle ways in which employers and employment agencies exclude Blacks, it becomes apparent in the existence of the many economic underachievers, unemployed, and welfare-supported families in the Black environment. Like the young Black male, they have had limited access to the job market and curtailed opportunities. Their presence declares that racism is a factor affecting whatever potential there is for achievement. Eventually the Black is awakened to the harsh reality that the combination of institutional factors—ghetto entrapment, his previous contacts with law enforcement agencies, and ghetto schools—come together to limit him from getting a job.

Thus racism not only plays a role in ghetto youths' lack of educational and vocational preparation but also ultimately defines the job world they can get into or aspire to. It also directly limits their knowledge of occupational options and their acquaintance with success models. Those who are continually forced to respond to and protect against acts of racism, because they are the constant objects of its processes, develop a whole range of behaviors to circumvent and ward off its impact. Defensive behavior such as limited investment in goal striving, limited aspirations, and assumption of a psychological readiness for failure are some of the devices employed. Many of these actions, and other "survivalistic" behaviors, ultimately reduce their intensity for achieving legitimate mainstream success. Activities taken to counter racism divert energy and attention away from more productive endeavors that could potentially provide greater social and personal benefits in the long run.

Hence institutional racism (which involves ghetto residence, inner-city educational institutions, police arrests, limited success models, undernourished aspirations, and limited opportunity) does not only produce lowered investment and increased self-protective maneuvers, it destroys motivation and, in fact, produces occupationally obsolete young men ready for underclass encapsulation.

In the end, the adjustments and adaptations that lower-class Blacks make to systematic rejection in order to survive—to find some source of income and to maintain individual integrity if possible—are formidable. However, as devices for achievement, many of these adaptations fail, not because of individual inadequacy or the lack of intense involvement, but rather because individual efforts are often impotent against the sum of systematic processes. The pervasiveness of racism in the world of jobs modifies the aspirations and job-seeking strategies of inner-city youth. Such modification, particularly that found in the search for alternative paths to achievement, is a significant variable affecting the mode and outcome of the economic strivings of Black youth.

The Daily Struggle

The trap in which these youths are caught cannot be fully understood in terms of theories, statistics, or comparison. It must be seen as a way of life, a constant struggle to deal with discrimination and rejection. It involves thinking about work and alternatives to working. If work is to be sought, it means figuring out how to circumvent being screened out. It involves going to the "man" in a sincere search for an opportunity to work, having only antiquated skills yet refusing to crawl. It involves a deep desire for work but requires modified emotional involvement in the search as a means of neutralizing the hurt of nonattainment. It means having high aspirations but having to find the ways to achieve them outside the mainstream. It involves feeling capable of handling the task if opportunity were available but believing the chances are limited. And it means facing the ultimate insecurity: That even when the job is secured, the job-holder must wonder not "What wages do I get?" but rather "How long can I fake and hold on until I learn or get fired?" As one of the men put it:

> Man, you jive your way in. I don't know nothing 'bout this job, but if I get a chance I'm sure I can do it. 'Cause see, I don't know what the man wants from me.

This struggle eventually becomes highly impersonal. The teacher, the rent collector, the police are seen as symbols of exclusion and limitation, not as positive social agents. The persons causing the condition of oppression are invisible, and thus the ghetto youths come up against cold institutions and procedures, computers programmed to reject those whose "social profiles" are characterized by having left school early and often by police records. The impersonal rejection is further exemplified by the functionally irrelevant and culturally discriminatory exams of employing agencies. The search for jobs, then, turns into a perpetual encounter with a world of institutional tricks, games, and deceit.

The futility of the ghetto youth's actions becomes apparent. By word of mouth he learns about some possibility—"if a brother gets a gig, then I run on down and see if I can pick up on a taste." (There is some truth in the overheard statement of an employer that "if you hire one, then they all begin to show up asking for some kind of a job.") But few of these leads materialize. Despair and cynicism grow as the fruitless routine of job-seeking gnaws away at endurance:

> I've been going to look for work in the morning, but you don't get shit. They always ask you for someone to reference for you, and then they find some excuse. If whitey be with you at the same time, then shit, bip-bap, and whitey gets the job.

The process continues for some for only a few months, and for others, years. The hostility against what is seen as systematic discrimination gains conscious meaning; the brother is ready for any game, almost any hustle. As was stated by one unemployed youth who had been this route and was now out of work for eight months:

> I was in training school, and looked for work in the mornings. I haven't found no work. Now, I'll be straight, I don't know where to turn. You do what's the next thing. If someone would tell me, like I'm ready.

Although profound obstacles stand in the way of job attainment, the young men also realized that they have contributed to their entrapment. Social scientists often refer to Black youths' self-destructive behavior, and it is apparent that the actions of the most excluded men frequently worsen their condition or intensify the problem of repair. Often when a young man hears of a potential job but has either failed to "take care of business" in the past or engaged in an activity that rules him out, particularly if the activity was not deemed crucial and was only done for kicks, he expresses regret. One of the older members of the study group, speaking of his chances for employment, reflected:

> I messed up some. I can't take it away, because I did it. But I know it's harder for me out there. Just try to get the job you want. White boys get the chance first.

Even in self-criticism, the ghetto reality of contending with favored competitors prevails.

In the typical sequence of events, the youth has aspirations and is motivated initially; then he "messes up," thus deep-

ening his exclusion; and finally after a period of years he becomes
so caught in the morass created by structural discrimination and
self-defeating behavior that he finds his perspectives are controlled by limited day-to-day survivalist activity. One of the
men on this downward spiral, when asked what affect being
Black had on his vocational obsolescence, replied:

> As for [being Black] being totally responsible,
> I couldn't say yes. Because of the things I have wanted,
> I haven't put forward all my effort. When I was younger,
> I had ambition. Now that I'm older, I have less, though
> I may get a chance.

Apparently the last potential for recovery is now lodged in
a "chance" factor; no more effort is to be expended on the
game. Still more unfortunate is the man who no longer even
hopes for a legitimate opportunity. Looking for work is entirely
a thing of the past "because I'm in and out of jail too much."
His struggle for economic survival has shifted to another arena,
the world of hustling, thugging, and burglary.

It is almost futile to argue which are more greatly hurt,
those who continue to try legitimate channels or those who
make themselves available for any game. However, if a distinction were made, the most tragic would probably be those who
are not even ready for any game—the street brothers, always
around, idly walking 103rd Street, in the Parking Lot, or on the
corner, without hope, beaten into submission. They no longer
give a damn; they refuse to search or even advertise that they
are available. They have lost faith in the social order, in those
who had promised some relief; they are skeptical of any change.
One such brother clearly states: "I haven't been trying. . . . If
people come up with something or I hear, I'll go. . . . If it's
straight, OK, or I'll leave it alone."

Nevertheless, the search for a job, for a way to make a living, for some money, consumes almost all the energy of most
ghetto youths. They have seen aspirations fail, know the skills
they possess are obsolete and unsalable. They have had at best

only limited low-level or part-time employment, and in many cases no work experience at all.

Because the barriers to success in the mainstream are largely beyond their control, the frenzied search for "bread," the struggle for survival, is shifted to the street milieu, the environment which appears to the entrapped ghetto youths to be at least open to influence. This is their turf, their community. The people here are good, and, they hope, the games are many. But owing to the community's meager resources, this turn is not likely to help them deal with their occupational obsolescence.

6

Adapting to Survival
on the Street

In Watts in the 1960s, perhaps most dramatic but most hidden
from public scrutiny were the young men aged fifteen through
thirty, physically healthy, alert, restive, and aggressively ready
for some action. But they were also economically obsolete. They
did not attend school, did not hold jobs, and even worse had no
real prospects for jobs in the future. In response to their exclusion, they first organized as roving, rival gangs, generally intimi-
dating the other citizens in the community. But as their condition of idleness and exclusion continued and no longer seemed
a temporary one, these young men organized a way of life to
secure some income and achieve some modicum of social pleasure. They gave up bopping and street rumbles and now sought
to be "ghetto sharp," to be mobile with a ride, and to get jobs
that paid good money. They wanted to be something.

By the time I had met the men of this study, they had
given up organized street fighting but continued to be known as
the most potentially explosive configuration in Watts. In the
community they were referred to as the Parking Lotters—a pseud-
onym for school dropouts, for jobless hoods. Of the eighty to
over one hundred young men who invariably hung out on the

Parking Lot in 1965, almost all were economically poor and were social rejects from various institutional programs. They formed one of the segments of the Watts underclass.

Subgroups in the Underclass

Young men who are removed at an early age from normal societal paths to economic security and to the attainment of a quality of life commensurate with the nation's capacity have a harrowing social and psychological existence. Each individual makes his own unique adjustment to the experience, yet because of the impact of being excluded early in life from normal social needs, and because of such common factors as deprivation and short-circuited opportunity, special group responses are developed to respond to the condition. This group of men made a particular adaptation to their social exclusion. The reaction was an aggressive approach to life, in large measure encouraged by their health and youth. Secondly, they used a deviant system to acquire money and a high-profile life-style as a way of demonstrating group membership and individual differences. Even though they were economically poor and had been characterized as failures by most institutions, they formed subgroups that adopted different roles and ways to express their survival adaptations.

Although these subgroups are not mutually exclusive, generally speaking, underclass young men responded in one of three ways to their designation as failures. Some accepted the label and adapted a passive posture in street life. In this category belong the steady drug users and winos, those who "be acting crazy" and end up in a mental institution or jail, or those who manage to stay on the streets and survive on some form of low-level hustling, begging, or handouts from residents. A second type of response involved those who retained some hope of limited mobility, usually expecting to reach this goal by acquiring a more or less permanent menial job, which if they were very fortunate would provide slow upgrading and salary increases after a long period. The aspirational commitments of those who adopt this strategy are invariably split between the inner-city and broader community. Although their social functioning is largely limited to the ghetto, they continue to strive for mainstream success and hope for a chance, a big break. They believe that one day, "I'm going to make it," that some occurrence will get them over to the other side. The third alternative, which was adopted by most of the men in this study, involves aggressive manipulation of the limited ghetto environment to maximize their social and economic potential. By the time I met then in 1965, the majority of the study group continued to believe that, given a chance, they could meet the requirements to obtain mainstream success. Whereas they had earlier held important aspirations for achievement, now they no longer aspired even to traditional lower-class jobs, much less to middle-class status. Psychologically, most were firmly committed to street culture, to making it any way they could. In short, their attitudes and practices were principally survivalistic. Those who periodically obtained entry into the legitimate work world—which usually consisted of marginal, seasonal, and dead-end jobs—were often motivated by the sheer weight of poverty or to display a semblance of commitment to a legitimate vocation, but most of their energy went into working some "hustle" in the streets.

Street culture, or the life in the enclave, is a special cultural environment. As discussed earlier, the whole large complex called the ghetto actually includes persons of all classes, but the streets—consisting of the small, lackluster bars, movie theaters, pawn shops, vacant lots, and in Watts a schoolyard intermeshed with the host of other marginal businesses—became the domain of this portion of the Watts underclass. This life, far from being the colorful experience implied by many studies, is both tedious and frenzied. As a means of socialization, it offers only a limited number of roles to local youngsters, particularly males. And of course, the more involved they are in street life, the more entrapped they become, seeking fulfillment in the few opportunities and roles available. They are all over each other trying to find some room and place for individual expression. Because of the meager means and resources of the ghetto, as well as its lack of internal controls, more intense activity is needed to produce immeasurably fewer results. Perpetual hustling—finding a way to get some money, some personal gratification is the pervasive mode of this existence.

Even so, young Blacks who grow up in the inner city seek social roles approximating those available to the majority in mainstream society, particularly those roles such as bankers, entrepreneurs, and information brokers that provide high status. Moreover, they demand that the range of material benefits available in the larger society be attainable by those in the ghetto, even though these may be in smaller portions and of inferior quality, or may have to be secured through illegitimate means. The young men are, in essence, continuing to pursue life aspirations, adopting those strategies that will permit them to achieve these goals through exploiting their limited environment to the maximum. Within these boundaries, success goes to those who are most cunning, able, and innovative in dealing with what is at hand. In some respects, then, street culture does not differ dramatically from mainstream life—both require intelligence and entrepreneurial skills. And both require personal energy and aggressiveness. *Hustling*, the term that has come to most aptly describe the daily concerns, psychology, and activity of the underclass Black, has several ramifications. There are *hustlers* —those who are the activists; *hustles*—the various games and opportunities; and, if one is most unfortunate and vulnerable, *being hustled*—being taken advantage of by someone else.

In the broadest sense, everyone in the ghetto is perceived as being involved in a hustle. Even the so-called legitimate Black storekeeper is viewed as having some hustle in order to keep his business going in the face of competition from more favored outsiders. Nevertheless, a special significance attaches to those young men who hustle the ghetto streets. These hustlers are arranged in a status hierarchy. In Watts in 1965, they were categorized as either players or activists. The player is described as being "sharp," well-polished, and as underplaying his skill rather than flaunting his attainment. He "knows all games" and "his is the greatest." He dresses well, possesses fine "threads." He is identifiable by his clean style and his accustomed dress—"slacks, suits, and hats"; he "ride his Cadillac." "He could fake good," and this made him a "righteous hustler." Faking well and being flexible are key characteristics of a "boss" player. It is clear that in most cases the player does not hold a legitimate job. As a matter of fact, he has open contempt for "heavy work," manual and dirty jobs. He views these as limited gigs with limited returns. However, he is not unalterably opposed on principle to temporary heavy work if it will lead to something greater. His source of income is rarely known, and although speculation abounds, the source is not as important as the fact that in appearance he is "making it."

The player can be found at different times in any of the ghetto systems, as he maintains contact with all levels of ghetto life and keeps open all avenues of communication. The player is "no dumb dude." He is highly articulate, bright, and conceptually oriented. His investment in the entire ghetto provides him with a comprehensive view of events. He is ambitious in that he seeks personal gain and status through clever manipulation of the environment. He assesses and makes judgments based on an astute grasp of ghetto psychology. His decisions are pragmatic—achieving goals is more important than adhering to any set of principles. In many respects he is the Machiavelli of the ghetto system. Operationally, he represents the functional intelligence of the streets. For all these reasons, he has come to be the ideal of many ghetto youth, particularly in the absence of other conspicuous, assertive, viable models of Black maleness. He outsmarts, outmanipulates the system of external limits placed on residents of the ghetto. He is cool!

In contrast to this cool player of all games is the activist, who obtains money through acts of vandalism, robbery, and theft. Within this category, there is a breakdown into "strong-arm studs," "stealers," and those who "rip off." These designations identify not only their methods but also the status of their activities. Some are "heavier" than others.

Strong-arm studs obtain money through acts of burglary and often use weapons. Since their object is cash, they concentrate on small stores, large businesses, and banks. In almost all cases they operate some distance outside the ghetto. Stealers differ from the strong-arm studs in that they do not necessarily use arms; they generally seek cash by indirect means—by selling or exchanging stolen goods—and their activities take place within the Black community, most often in the bordering neighborhoods of the ghetto. The objects of their theft are household appliances, furniture, and clothing: items that are scarce in the poverty-ridden section of the ghetto and will therefore bring a good price.

Unlike the previously noted schemes, ripping-off requires little, if any, planning; it is engaged in spontaneously, as opportunity arises. The rip-off man does not care much what objects he takes or where, as long as they seem to be usable or salable. In some cases, he does not know their value, and his ripping off rarely provides any significant income. It sometimes supplements other sources, but the greatest attraction of this practice is that it reinforces the belief that chance or good luck can still prevail. Clearly, the activist receives less prestige and less usable income than does the player. And the more openly illegal actions result in many arrests and jailings, and they do provide some income for large numbers of poor men in a limited economic system.

Another hustle, one that has gained much attention from some special social investigators, is the practice of securing "broad money." Various studies have closely linked or identified this practice with pimping. However, although pimping certainly exists in street culture, the term does not properly characterize the relationships between most of these underclass Black males and their female companions. Anyone examining these relationships undoubtedly recognizes some special patterns different from those of working- and middle-class Blacks. The major element is the intensity of the underclass male's economic exclusion and deprivation and consequent economic impotence in a materially oriented society. Not only is he unable to occupy the approved role of breadwinner for a woman or family, but he cannot even generate any continuous income for his own subsistence. Thus he becomes dependent on the underclass woman, who has at least a few more ways to get money, often from low-paid jobs in mainstream society. She can secure an income through industrial or domestic employment, welfare, and sometimes prostitution. Consequently, in the poorest Black families, the woman very often makes most of the money. (As noted earlier, even in middle-class families, where the male is slowly becoming able to earn an increasingly steady income, female wages are usually needed to support a middle-class standard of life.)

The male who receives financial support from women, particularly in an extremely complex relationship, carries varying obligations, promises, and expectations. In most cases, he is expected to be a dependable sexual partner and protector. Having a steady man is an important measure of femininity in street culture; and it also provides protection, reducing the amount of "hitting on" (sexual aggression) to which the female is exposed. Further, the man may be expected to act as a surrogate father, a masculine symbol to his partner's children, and to supply social companionship, especially on those occasions when it is inappropriate for a female to be present or involved without a man. Perhaps most important, having "a man around the house" keeps alive for all the reality of a complete union and family, as well as the hope for a more stable family one day. It also gives some credence to the lingering dream of successful mobility with an achieving man.

When the men in the study group fulfilled these expectations, they achieved mutually satisfying relationships with their women most of the time. In such alliances, the fact that they were receiving financial support was not a denigrating factor; it was usually understood as part of the female's commitment to the partnership. But when the men approached women with the attitude of solely getting "broad money," of manipulating them in a game that had little to do with promising stability or being committed to a relationship, the consequences were quite different. To gain access to this steady source of income, some of these men postured as good bedmen, studs, and good-time dudes. It was clear that they could be purchased without any major commitment, and thus most of their contacts involved short-term ties and the provision of services to the loneliest or newest females in the community. These men developed a psychology to support their behavior. Some rationalized that they were a needed commodity in the streets; they insisted they were not pimping. Others used bravado to maintain their function, continually speaking of their sexual prowess. Despite peer support for these roles, most of these men were constantly on the move, ducking and being searched for by one or another female, as some aspect of the "contracted" relationship was either violated or assumed to be so. Thus, their manipulative attitudes provided the primary basis for the prevailing conflict between the men and women of the Watts underclass. Another drawback of securing broad money for survival was that the actual amount of money they managed to secure was so infinitesimal that even when they squeezed a few dollars from some women, the men ultimately experienced their impotence: They had the lingering sense of having achieved "no big thing," since the real source of deprivation, the larger society, still excluded them. They had come no closer to escaping the ghetto and, in most cases, only became more trapped by the daily hassling that resulted from their mercenary involvement.

The women's money itself comes, as noted earlier, from various marginal and sometimes steady but lower-income jobs and more importantly from the welfare system. Owing to the severe poverty in the ghetto, huge sums flow in from this latter source, and many no- and low-income Black families are tied to it. Although the payments made to individuals and their families provide only a bare existence, it has become the most stable income source for many underclass people. For this reason, the first and the fifteenth of each month are now institutionalized happenings in the ghetto. On these days bills can be paid, indebtedness is temporarily lessened, and a few things that bring some relief from deprivation are secured. During these short periods, there is money in the streets, and the men who have a connection to this source get to it.

Another activity that has received considerable notice is drug trafficking. Many social scientists, as well as the general public, believe there is a large flow of drugs in the ghetto and infer that it provides a major income source for young ghetto dwellers. But while it is true that the ghetto population is widely vulnerable to drugs, the majority of the men in the Watts study group were not hard drug users. And although the drug system was well known to them, partly because of openness of

its operations and partly because of its evident destructive effects on good people, young as well as old, these men put down
the culture of drugs. They recognized that the system could
bring in "good money," but they did not see it as a genuine
opportunity system, since it was believed (in Watts in 1965)
to be controlled by outside forces, usually identified as "Mafia
people."*

Most Blacks who are involved today, particularly those
who handle the movement of drugs within the ghetto, are not
considered any different from the Blacks who showcase for the
legitimate white institutions within the ghetto. It is maintained
that although these "front men" get some good bread, they
have no control or influence in the organizations that run ghetto
drug operations. Unlike so many other practices that persist in
the ghetto, drug trafficking is judged negatively, as it is considered dangerous to controlled survival. Those who use drugs
are considered personally undependable, at best, and likely to
stimulate police harassment for everyone. In short, drug operations are a totally "bad news scene for the folks."

Among the men in the study, drug use was limited mostly
to smoking marijuana which, incidentally, was not considered
a drug. "Firing a joint" was usually a social activity, although
some brothers were seen to be high at times when no group use
had taken place. In 1966–1967, some of the men also "dropped
pills," barbiturates and amphetamines such as Seconal and Ben-
zedrine (usually called "reds" and "bennies"). These pills, also
sometimes referred to as dope, were not widely used because of
their scarcity and cost. LSD, with which many white youths
were experimenting in the sixties, was not deemed worth the
trip in Black areas. The Watts men looked upon it as being as
dangerous as heroin, for the user became "wasted," often lost
control, and thereby threatened the requisite self-control and
"cool."

*Although this was the prevailing belief then, more recent dis-
closures by Congressional investigation committees note that ghetto drug
traffic is now directly in the hands of Black-controlled narcotics organizations. However, the broader national and international management of
illegal drugs continues to be in the hands of non-Blacks.

In general, the underclass males' relation to drug trafficking somewhat resembled their relation to other economic systems, principally the legitimate job world. The drug trade was reputedly able to provide "long bread," good money, but only for a few. The typical study group member could not gain access to the controlling positions or to the big sums collected daily. For him, even if he became a pusher, the drug system would never be a major source of income. As usual, he held options at the bottom of the pole, either as a user or one able to be manipulated by outsiders. In respect to drug use, his major concern was finding a way to ease the pain of daily living, to get a "hum" and a little "high," without losing control, which would be antithetical to ghetto functioning.

Socialization: Learning Survival Ways

As we have seen, street culture is a principal agent of socialization for the underclass young male, although it offers only a few roles and provides limited opportunity for variations. Differences in social status are therefore based largely on the individual's ability to develop a distinctive style rather than on displays of material possessions. Those roles allowed are highly ritualized, and individual innovation as manifested through personalized styling alone makes for subtle variations; thus, the walk, manner of speech, choice of "threads," hairdo (natural or processed), and, above all else, "maintaining one's cool" take on inordinate importance. From early adolescence, the young spend each day developing the nuances, the subtleties, that will earn them the reputation of being "down" instead of "square," one of the "ins," not one of the "outs." As in circumscribed subcultures, being "in" and conforming to specified patterns of behavior validate the person's commitment to the culture and permit his functioning in it.

Street life teaches that the vital aspect of the male's image is his "cool," even under the most adverse of conditions. Maintaining cool is not merely stylistic, however; ultimately it has a great deal to do with developing a sense of dignity and worth. Since there are so few symbols with which to augment his image—no $90,000 home, Brooks Brothers suit, or original painting—all the man is must be conveyed in human encounters. His peers judge him accordingly: "The cat's beautiful," or "He ain't shit." Because cool is such an essential attribute and maintaining it has such an important effect on his ego, the ghetto youth would sooner go down than blow his cool, even in a situation where he has to retreat and the particular game is considered lost. The loss is not catastrophic if the brother is able to negotiate the situation and maintain control and his self-respect. Cool involves showing that he knows what's happening and has the ability to act in appropriate ways. It further involves being tough and not easily persuaded. These qualities were illustrated in a story told by one of the men. The actions of the story's subject might appear to be a parody on the heroic-struggle-against-great-odds theme, but they were actually necessary for ego survival.

> A brother was hemmed in by twenty-five cops and the dude didn't have nothing with him, and knew that them motherfuckers was going to head whip him. Man, that brother didn't move back an inch. He just put up his dukes, and went at them cops with their carbines and shotguns and riot sticks. Man, they beat the shit out of him, man messed him all up—but that brother was cool. Good brother.

Clearly peer acclaim for, and sanction of, the young Black's performance strengthens his functioning. Thus his identity is molded and validated by the brother on the street.

Another important aspect of socialization is learning to rap well, to be a clever and effective manipulator of person and environment. In a situation where one must aggressively manipulate a hostile environment in order to force it to meet one's needs, even one's friends are subject to being "faked," "gamed," or "hit on." Therefore the relations between peers are intense, guarded, and competitive, and much interaction involves "faking," "hitting-on," and "running a game" as a way of validating the strength of the other's position. The medium for this assessment is rapping.

Although the written word—the Black Panther press, materials on Afro development in *Jet*, and the writings of Malcolm X, Mohammed, Rap Brown, and the new Black poets— acquired some vogue in the sixties, verbal communication remained a primary means of socialization for the underclass male. In this way he not only tests his competitors but exchanges ideas and learns how to behave as a member of street culture. Much time is thus spent in perfecting character by exploring all aspects of life. Hour after hour of "bullshit" is what the perpetual argumentative discussions appear to be. In these debates every and any subject is material for discourse, so long as it involves a certain degree of controversy. Once the issue is identified, sides are taken. Neither personal experience nor formal knowledge qualifies one as an expert; the winner is determined by his verbal dexterity and impressive personality and these are expressed in his style of presentation. The rapping usually occurs between two persons at a time, while the other group members observe. These arbiters establish the rules, act as judges of Black character and Black style, and ultimately determine whether there is a victor. A winner is not easily determined, and the group is not hasty in deciding, since the substance of the debate may be secondary to its socialization function. Very often when the protagonists are "beautifully" engaged, the observers encourage them by interjecting opinions, "signifying," and generally abdicating their role as arbitrators, while exhorting the protagonists to demonstrate their ability.

As the debate goes on, the original issue may be supplemented by another or be totally forgotten; content is not as important as developing form and style. Because each protagonist invests so much of his ego in the process, he defends his position every way he can. In the absence of objective evidence on the subject, he resorts to argumentative devices designed to lessen the integrity, credibility, and personal respect of his opponent in the eyes of the observers. Appeals for points, "scores," are directed not so much to the opponent as to the audience. The personal reputations of the two competitors are at stake. To disagree or to hold a varying opinion is to attack the integrity and personal worth of the supporter. Eloquent verbosity is augmented by artful prancing, significant body positioning, and gesticulation. Although the literature continues to cite the limited language skills of Black youth, in these situations there is no dearth of verbal skills, particularly in use of Black dialect. The ability to think on one's feet and come up with creative phrases spontaneously earns support from the uncommitted and weakens the opponent's position.

To end these often heated exchanges is sometimes no simple matter. In a more formal debate it is possible to reach a conclusion by consulting some objective authority or source of reliable information. But in this situation, if the "hassle" is good, the supposed external authorities—the peer observers—may also become participants, and this makes it difficult to stop. The rap may end when one person "cops out," when the two agree to stop (a rarity), when a third party intervenes (demanding that the two "stop the bullshit"), or, as often occurs, when the whole encounter is reduced to physical threat or confrontation. Of course if "something's happening" down the street or uptown, this takes immediate precedence, since this is what so much of the culture is about: "waiting for something to happen."

Organizational Influences: Focus on Law Enforcement

The young man growing up in the streets is also shaped by the many institutions and organizations that structure ghetto life. Although in the early years of Watts there was a paucity of support groups, as indicated in Chapter Three, by 1965 a number of Black-controlled organizations had developed some influence. Among those in Los Angeles were the Black church (particularly the storefront, Pentecostal, and small Baptist denominations); various local and sometimes statewide social-betterment groups; the social club network, including formal sports organizations; and those organizations that sprang from the community's sociopolitical concerns—the Black Panthers and the Muslims, for instance (the latter was both a religious and political group). The formal and informal communication networks were significant as well. Black newspapers (the *Afro,*

Currier, Chronicle, and *Sentinel)* and Black radio (usually found between 1300 and 1600 on the dial) existed in tandem with the street system, in which information passed (often more quickly and effectively) among bars, restaurants, barber shops, and beauty parlors. All of these systems were an important part of the inner-city institutional network. But their impact was small in contrast with that of the white-run institutions and services, such as the schools, the health care system, the public utilities, the social services network, the government antipoverty programs, and, prominently, the system of law enforcement. Although some Blacks worked in these mainstream-controlled institutional systems, they were almost never in policy-making positions.

As the ghetto dweller sees it, these organizations negatively control ghetto life and serve the community with disdain. And, furthermore, they appear to be almost impervious to change. At best, they are considered necessary evils, to be manipulated for personal advantage whenever possible. The ghetto youth's contacts with these externally run networks begin early and are experienced negatively. The school programs are alien and unfair. The food markets and small stores, which are dirty and sell low-grade products, also hold indebtedness, since purchases are made on credit, "put on the book." The public welfare system is experienced as oppressive, because it controls such an important source of income and demands that recipients meet what are considered to be unrealistic requirements. Then there are the irregular garbage collections, the utility companies that threaten to cut off electricity or water or that dig holes in the middle of the street and leave garbage baskets in them overnight. But the organization that arouses the most hate is the law enforcement system, represented primarily by the police.

This institution has done more to unify the sentiments of ghetto youth concerning social codes, laws, and concepts of justice than any other agency encountered by poor Blacks. From a very young age, ghetto males develop an antipathy to the police. At first there is fear, which is followed by suspicion and, ultimately, hatred. Police are seen as bandits, thugs, and "head whippers," whose behavior is sanctioned by the broader community. Although they are public servants, ghetto citizens feel they have no control over police actions and no means to gain redress. The manner in which the police function is such that the entire Black community is very ambivalent about whether the practice of saturating the central city with police officers deters crime or creates worse conditions due to increased antagonism between the police and local citizens. In the ghetto, the police are sought only in situations of extreme necessity.

Every young man who grows up in the inner-city ghetto can expect to have some confrontation with the police. He may be chased for playing ball in "prohibited" areas (in the streets), as well as for minor theft. He experiences the intimidation of being "busted"—apprehended and questioned. Feeling securely backed by their powerful officialdom, and encouraged by the poor Blacks' lack of machinery for responding to injustice, the police perpetuate a system of harassment and dehumanization. The main target of this denigrative process is the young male. He is made to feel unprotected, vulnerable in his own neighborhood, always subject to questioning; he is suspected of every crime and made to prove his innocence in every encounter. This process results in numerous arrests and citations, since almost all ghetto poor are at some time in minor violation of the law or may be implicated by past arrests.

The police strategy is twofold: control and containment. The control function—involving busts, arrests, and general rousting—is carried out primarily within the ghetto. Containment involves the harassment of young Blacks, particularly males, found in bordering non-Black communities. These encounters do not consist of subtle dehumanization but sheer intimidation: the police stop the man and demand to know why he is there and where he is going. If a satisfactory response is given (that is, satisfactory to the police officer), the person may be allowed to proceed; if not, he is arrested, usually as a suspect, and searched. In essence, the youth is made to justify his presence in an area that is public but white.

These sorts of confrontations were commonly experienced by the men in the study group, especially in the early periods of the development of Watts, Compton, and Willowbrook. In fact, almost every one of them had been busted at least once. One of the married men described an encounter he had had while driving home with his wife:

> We were coming home late one night and we saw the man in his car following us, so we just kept driving right. At the red light, they pulled up beside our car and both of them sat there staring at us. I knew that they wanted to do something, so I just looked at them and turned away and went on talking with my wife. So at the next light they pulled up again and this time put the spotlight in the car. So I was angry now and rolled down the window and said, "What you shining that light on us for?" Man, that cracker jumped out of his car, gun drawn, and shouting, "come on, nigger, get out that car." They asked for license, searched the trunk, pulled up the back seat of the car, asked my wife what she was doing with me, and who she were. All the time they tore up the car, they kept on telling me, "stand still, nigger, don't you move; get over there or we mess you up." Then they gave me a ticket for the glass of the back light was missing.

In situations like this, the police not only depreciate the woman but use her presence to provoke the man into a protective reaction that will give them an excuse "to bust up the brother." Men have been beaten, shot, and jailed because they responded to harassment by demanding respect for their women. The charge in these cases is "resisting arrest" or something similar. To justify the charge, the police may say the man made "a menacing movement with his hands," an allegation that has been popular in many cases.

In addition to dehumanizing the victims, the busting reinforces the image of the police officers' complete and unquestionable control. The personal insults and threats cannot be challenged without precipitating a "head busting," if not more severe treatment. The alternative is to pursue the issue in court, where racial discrimination and the power structure favoring the police are sure to bring defeat again. On the basis of much firsthand experience, the study men felt there was no legal way to redress their grievances against the police. The humiliation they experienced in these encounters cannot be measured in terms of time lost, inconvenience, simple fright; it must be seen in terms of damage to human integrity and maleness.

The busting often has further injurious consequences as well. As is shown in the example just quoted, if a man reacts in any way or if some violation is exposed during search and questioning, he is arrested and booked—his name is taken, and he is fingerprinted and questioned about his living situation. This arrest record is then used by social institutions to deprive the youth of opportunities, particularly employment. Additionally, if the man is brought to trial and sentenced and serves time in jail, upon release he must navigate the probation period. During this time, he cannot take certain types of jobs, and he becomes even more vulnerable to police, who can threaten to take him in for probation violation. The study men did state that their probation officers were the single official contact in the law enforcement system that was often understanding and helpful. Every other member of the system was considered to be out to get them. The police have earned their infamy among these young men who have never known the "good officers" who guide children safely across the street.

Yet as intense as the anger is concerning law enforcement and the other institutions controlled by the broader society, these ghetto youth maintain an envy toward the effectiveness and pervasiveness of this persecuting machinery. There is little doubt that they are angry at the world of "whitey," the world that surrounds them in seeming luxury and plenty and denies them by putting them in the "trick bag" of ghetto living. In their minds, poverty, unemployment, and the constellation of deprivation in which they are caught is the result not of chance but of deliberate disqualification, deceit, racism, and the use of power by "the man." It is this perception that arouses an almost envious deference to white power, its organization, its ability to fulfill its purpose, and its magnitude. The concept of "the man's machine" is used to explicate the interconnected effectiveness of coordinated actions. The white power structure is viewed as being "no fool." Far from being crude, it shows an unwavering cleverness and commitment to reaching its goals, one of which is to keep Blacks in a state of disunity and disorganization. As one brother noted:

> First thing, is the man had boxed them [Blacks] in; you see how he's fixed everything so he can't lose; whitey is smart, nobody's fool. He gets the brothers to fight each other, when all the time he's out there behind it.

Despite the assessed strength and cunning of mainstream institutions, however, the young men did not adopt an acquiescent posture of helplessness. They responded with spirited antagonism, seeking ways to deal with, "destroy," and "whip" the man's machine. Thus, deeply enmeshed in ghetto life, these underclass men become governed chiefly by the daily rituals of survival. They are socialized to know where to go for what, how to obtain what is not normally available, and whom they should know to get what they need—all in a system of depleted means. No fanciful detention centers "secretly being built to harbor niggers" could be worse than the reality of the modern ghetto trap. The resentment originally generated by the mass white exodus has long since subsided, and for at least ten years the central city has been all Black. Many of the encounters, tensions, and survival struggles involve Blacks with Blacks. The truth is that no one is spared the destructive consequences of ghetto living. The never-ending cycle goes something like this: Being broke, hustling, jiving, stealing, rapping, balling; a fight; a bust, some time; no job, lost a job, a no-paying job; a lady, a baby, some weight; some wine, some grass, a pill; no ride, lost pride, man going down, slipping fast, can't see where to make it; I've tried, almost died, ready now for almost anything.

7

From Futility
to Rebellion

Finally in 1965 the young men of Watts exploded. Why? Considerable debate has taken place on this question, and much has been written as well. Although some analysts suggested this rebellion was a conspiracy directed at embarrassing the country, and others tried to minimize its importance by terming it an isolated antisocial act of "unreachable youth" who had no interests in common with other Blacks or mainstream society, wiser heads cited the deep economic and psychological sources of the outbreak: poverty, racial discrimination, long-term isolation from the broader society, and the resultant anger and frustration—a whole accumulation of causes that have been investigated in this book. These factors do not tell us, however, why it happened when it did and why in Watts.

Certainly an important influence on the timing was the Civil Rights Movement. Most of the study men stated that it was a "hopeless cause"—the marching, the sit-ins, all the work to break open and prick the conscience of a racist system—yet within themselves they still hoped that some change would occur. But soon this small hope waned and was replaced by anger

105

when the men saw the southern whites' reactions to the marchers and sit-in demonstrators. Daily these men mulled over what
they had observed on television the night before or heard on the
early morning news. Young and old Blacks were being whipped,
stoned, cursed and beaten, jailed and humiliated; and what was
most antithetical to the style of the Watts men, the Civil Rights
marchers never fought back, "never got one." The men resolved
that they would never passively accept this treatment from the
"man." In other words, the Movement raised their hopes and
expectations without fulfilling them. Whereas earlier they had
turned much of their anger in on themselves—fighting, community vandalism, gang confrontation—simmering in their own juices,
as it were, their rage and resentment now arose to a new high
and was externalized. Some also felt, that the Reverend Martin
Luther King, Jr., and his supporters were too oriented toward
integration. Additionally, Watts lacked traditions or structures
to absorb racially produced anger. Compared to the southern
Blacks' world, California is less structured, uncontrolled, and
not easily contained.

The ghetto seethed, tensions mounted, and the police—
the hated symbol of Black containment in enclaves north and
south—finally provided the catalyst that set in motion one of
the most ravaging outbursts of Blacks in the history of this nation. Their rage was directed at white society's structure, its
repressive institutions and their symbols of exploitation in the
ghetto: the chain stores, the oligopolies that control the distribution of goods; the lenders, those who hold the indebtedness
of the ghetto bound; the absentee landlords; and the agents who
control the underclass while safeguarding the rights of those
who exploit it. The explosion was intended to get even with
those whom poor Blacks hate and resent, the people who profit
from the powerless condition of the poor and the entrapped; it
also represented their hope of making some change in their living conditions.

These then, were the broad causes of the Watts rebellion.
The immediate spark was an all-too-familiar occurrence: a "black
and white" (patrol car) apprehending with force just one more

young Black. The story has been told many times (Cohen, 1970; McCone, 1965); there is nothing in the accounts of those eventful days that needs to be reiterated. However, it should never be forgotten that the actual destruction, turmoil, and community immobilization were precipitated by a relatively small number of young and poor, but volatile, persons. And although most studies focus on the impact that these young men had on the workings of the city, little attention has been given to understanding the effect that participation in the rebellion had on the individuals themselves. We know from the usual statistical information that many were hurt, some incarcerated, and some even killed, but what has been omitted from scrutiny is the real human drama of the surviving participants and the effect that this involvement had on their future lives. A different approach is needed to answer the question of what propelled a young man in 1965 to throw a blazing bottle of gasoline into a storefront in the late afternoon when only hours earlier he was with a friend at the beach making love. And it is more important to ascertain what encouraged the same young man to move from violence and destruction to activities for community improvement, all within the short period of six months. In the end we must ask what were the social mechanisms making such dramatic movement possible—from violence to constructive involvement, from gang hooliganism to responsible participation. These changes began for many of these men on the evening of August 11, when a California highway patrolman, Lee W. Minkus, gave chase and pulled over the car of twenty-one-year-old Marquette Frye and his brother Ronald, twenty-two. The officer, concerned with reckless driving, administered a sobriety test, which Frye failed. Frye was arrested, while his brother sought out their mother in order to secure the automobile. During these events, a crowd of 250 to 300 persons gathered, and exchanges ensued between the arrested man, the patrolman, and the watching crowd. The details of what happened next are disputed, but the general sequence went something like this: the crowd began to throw rocks. A patrolman was injured; other police were called in. The local residents came into the streets in a reaction to the police show of strength, and soon a pitched battle was under way.

The many displaced, forgotten, voiceless, "unreachables" also took to the streets, throwing off the constraints that had held them in for so long. This became possible as these most isolated young men were no longer alone, for they were joined by people from almost every section of the Watts community, who either took an active part—looting and resisting the police action —or gave their tacit support by becoming emotionally identified with those in the streets. Estimates of the number of Blacks actively involved in what was in 1965 named "the Watts riot" range as high as ten thousand. And before the crisis in Watts was officially considered ended, almost every Black in Los Angeles was at least implicated, since more than four hundred thousand (about two thirds of the Black population of Los Angeles) were confined to their communities by a curfew enforced by the National Guard and the police. The statistics compiled by the McCone committee (McCone, 1965, pp. 23–25) give a further indication of the scope of the community rebellion:

> There were thirty-four persons killed and 1,032 reported injuries. . . . 118 of the injuries resulted from gunshot wounds. . . . The Coroner's jury ruled that twenty-six of the deaths were justifiable homicide, five were homicidal, and one was accidental. Of those ruled justifiable homicide, the jury found that death was caused in sixteen instances by officers of the Los Angeles Police Department and in seven instances by the National Guard. . . .
>
> Between 2,000 and 3,000 fire alarms were recorded during the riot. . . . There were 3,438 adults arrested, 71 percent for burglary and theft. . . . [The number] of juveniles arrested was 514, 81 percent for burglary and theft. . . . During the riots, law enforcement officers recovered 851 weapons. . . .
>
> [Property damage was estimated at more than $40,000,000.] More than 600 buildings were damaged by burning and looting. Of this number, more than 200 were totally destroyed by fire. The rioters concentrated primar-

ily on food markets, liquor stores, furniture stores, clothing stores, department stores, and pawn shops. . . . No
residences were deliberately burned; damages to schools,
libraries, churches, and public buildings were minimal;
and certain types of business establishments—notably service stations and automobile dealers—were for the most
part unharmed. . . . [Further], there was no evidence that
the rioters made any attempt to steal narcotics from
pharmacies in the explosive area even though some pharmacies were looted and burned.

This pattern of burning, in which certain businesses and institutions were spared while their next door neighbors were hit full
force, suggested to the press and to some Blacks that the riot
had been planned. But the participants did not confirm this
view. The rebellion was not organized, either by Black power
radicals or militant street brothers. The pattern developed spontaneously as a common reaction to a common experience—
their manipulation by representatives of the mainstream and
their inability to mask and suppress the indignities as a community.

Participation of the Men from the Study Group

In all that was printed about this event, only a few reports
sought to convey the participants' attitudes and depth of feeling, and even fewer dealt with the effects of taking part in this
social holocaust on the activists and survivors. Therefore, let us
go back and look closely at the experiences of the study men.
Before the summer of 1965, as we have seen, these youths were
known to the community as the incorrigible thugs, hustlers, and
bad dudes from the Parking Lot, sometimes dubbed "the Cons
of the Stronghold." In social science parlance, they were characterized as classically antisocial. Many had extensive police records, some were recognized cogs in the ghetto criminal system,
and some even had been imprisoned many times. Most also had
been unemployed for a long time and had never experienced
socially productive roles since leaving high school. A few in the

group had not yet developed such clearly obsolete social profiles, as they were newly out of school and only discovering for
the first time their inability to secure employment. They could
not be accurately characterized as hard-core yet, but they were
already showing the familiar ingredients—educational termination, unemployment, no salable skills, no supportive institutional contacts, closed mobility, and no future. They had gravitated
to the Parking Lot because it offered them a place. Thus, the
new arrivals and the older members were all linked together,
and their future societal worth was questionable at best. They
were destined to function as a part of the Watts underclass.

For the young men of the Stronghold the hot day of
August 11 began like all other days, nothing special, nothing
unique. They were just hanging-out when they heard the word.
One young man recalled how he started out almost like an observer:

> I was sitting in the Lot and we heard there was
> a stoning. Some patty got stoned. His eye was hanging
> out. It started so damn fast; it didn't look like a riot. It
> started in Compton by a group of guys we hadn't even
> seen before. . . .
> Seems like some patty studs were jumped on; then
> brother studs looked like they were looking for any white
> guys. We stood there looking for the cops to come, but
> nobody came.
> Then the buses of "black and white" came, and got
> rocked; then other buses came; and the cops got out one
> at a time, and they got rocked. This happened in one
> group. The police reacted at everybody, plus the innocent.
> Montgomery was still on their minds. Then mom and the
> grandfathers began throwing stones, because of the hid-
> den anger. . . . At the height of it—word went out, we was
> going to fuck up Watts.

Others thought it was just another happening:

> I didn't think too much of it at first, just thought
> it was a few dudes getting it together. I didn't feel the im-
> pact until later when the burning began to take place.

Or in the words of another:

> No, I didn't think anything about it. I was just angry at
> the P.D.; that's why I came off the Lot. I didn't know it
> was happening like it was.

None of those who participated did so with prethought or plan.
They were initially just curious bystanders looking to see what
was happening.

Some were not even in the area when the explosion started.
One young man who later became an active rebeller was at the
beach with some girlfriends. As he approached Avalon on the
way home, he saw what he thought was about 150 policemen.
He remembered:

> The people seemed to have the upper hand, and
> I felt inspired to see the P.D. run instead of the people. . . .
> It was like excitement behind a holiday or how young
> kids feel at Christmas. I've never experienced it before,
> and I couldn't hardly believe it. It seemed like a dream.
> There were so many L.A.P.D., the largest in the country
> in trying to stop crime, and they just stood there, and me
> picking up stuff—stuff that would take fifteen years to
> get, I got in one day.

Thus, their bystander status changed with electrifying quickness
to identification with events and then to involvement when the
word went out that the police had jacked up another brother
and his mother. Another man explained how he got caught up
in the action:

> I was coming home, when everyone was looting.
> I came from the dentist and saw Martin's burning—flames.
> I felt that I wanted to get even with the white folks; I took,
> and I got even. I was a bit scared and the police hemmed
> me up—I talked peace talk until my boys came, then we
> split.

Although much has been written about the shocked responses of the white community, not reported was the conta-

gious involvement of Blacks, even those who were unable to make it into Watts during the riot. One of the Parking Lot men who was then incarcerated remembered the preparations undertaken by prison authorities to keep the information away from the prisoners

> We didn't know about what was happening at first. They kept it a secret; they even changed the prison routine. On the third day we finally saw it on TV. Most of the "bloods" wanted to riot then. Whitey was nervous.

Another in a different jail recalled his frustration at not being able to be with the brothers in Watts. He recounts the excitement of the inmates when they finally heard the news:

> The brothers got together. I was hollering, "Burn, Baby, Burn." Lou Rawls expressed it well: "Tear it up, blow it up, Tobacco Road, and build it up again". This was the feeling I had. I wanted to destroy and rebuild. I wish I was there, but I was in jail.

The motivations and feelings of the men who were in the rebellion varied significantly. In the midst of ripping off goods, surrounded by a burning community, many were afraid. Some were concerned for persons they loved and at the same time were pulled by the chance to fulfill their own longing for a suit, a pair of shoes, a saxaphone. Others hoped to maintain their status as "together" brothers in the eyes of their peers yet feared the real possibility of being killed, for the police were out in force and shotting to kill. So some participated with bravado, others with a cool determination to even the score, and still others with deep fears of personal destruction.

One young man who was active the first evening, and who came back the next day, remembered the unreal quality of the event and his participation:

> Man, it was strange. The sky was red, and the sun looked like it would never set. Everything was free. And cars was burning, and white people being tossed back in-

to the burning car. And clothes piled up so high, suits, guitars—man, just unreal. I was arrested, stealing too fast.

Others experienced this sense of unreality, as they became involved in an unprecedented event; the traditional social limits were absent—for a while there was a state of normlessness. One described this experience in very global terms:

> I thought the world was coming to an end . . . uncontrolled . . . lost control . . . a truly unreal situation. Man, mad, unreal.

Some felt excited by the material possibilities. One youth, affected by marked deprivation, noted unrealistically:

> For a while during the riots, I thought I'd get rich just by looting.

Others were exhilarated by the sense of freedom, as an older man noted:

> During the riot, I felt free, but I kept my cool. I felt that it had to happen—we just had to show the people what was happening.

Still others had mixed feelings.

> Man, you must be kidding. It was the greatest thing ever happened to me. We got whitey; we got some P.D., and we got all kinds of things. I know guys who ripped off whole racks of suits, and ten and twelve pairs of shoes. . . . It may happen again if things don't change. I hope it don't, 'cause so many people got hurt. And no food for days, no stores or. . . . Old people were afraid, and some kids were afraid. I know some guys the P.D. beat the shit out of when they caught them. *It was no picnic, but we had a ball.*

On the third day of the rebellion, some persons became aware of another kind of unreality: a change in community

power. The control seemingly had shifted from the law enforcement officials to the people. For some this produced an increased
sense of purpose; for others it aroused great uneasiness:

> I was scared! It was like [long pause] a jar of mar-
> bles dropped and it broke loose. It was a great confusion.
> I was confused as to what was happening. The first day of
> the riot, there was looting and stores broken into. At first
> there were not too many people on the streets. . . . Then
> they started coming. The police on the street tried to di-
> rect traffic and the people just went around him. The cop
> threw up his hands—what the hell—and the people just
> did what they wanted. Then more and more people—
> cars, kids, everything was wild. I was scared . . . grabbed
> my brother . . . went home. I had a funny feeling . . .
> I couldn't go . . . I feared being shot.

Another, whose excitation drove him into the streets
rather than to his home, recalled:

> It was strange. I did what I did, but sometimes it
> was like it weren't me. I cared, but then I didn't worry
> about nothing on the second day. Then I was arrested;
> the P.D. lined up a whole lot of guys. They had shot guns
> and pistols and everything. They wanted to shoot. Next
> thing, we were in jail. It was different from anything else
> I've known. Wild, man, just wild.

Thus, the degree and kind of involvement in this social upheaval
differed for each man, yet it had a lasting impact on all of them
and molded their future role as a group.

The rebellion was severely curtailed on August 14 when
Governor Pat Brown sealed off a 250-square-mile area of Los
Angeles, putting the majority of the Black residents of Los Angeles under a restrictive curfew. The crisis was considered officially ended on August 17, when the governor lifted the curfew. Almost as imperceptibly as the rebellion had begun, it
ended. The police finally gained control of the streets; mass
arrests had resulted in many of the rebels being jailed. The fires

in the ghetto were extinguished as the firemen obtained unimpeded access to burning buildings. The whole might of the state —the police, National Guard, and special armed forces—was mobilized to crush the rebellion. But the issues, of course, were far from closed. In fact this community's rebellion had only opened the books, exposing many issues needing review.

Reactions and Assessment

It was shocking to realize that such a relatively small group of people could generate so much activity and gain the attention of the whole nation. Obviously, the scope of their rebellion surpassed that of any earlier outburst in U.S. ghettos. It cost more, aroused a greater mainstream response, involved a larger number and a broader cross-section of Blacks, and was directed against different objects. Notably undermentioned in the reports was the significant fact referred to at the beginning of the chapter: that the object of their anger was the institutional fabric of the ghetto, not, as was traditional in earlier riots, individual white citizens. Therefore, in this confrontation between Blacks and whites, the white participants were the agents of the broader community: the police, National Guardsmen, officials of various government agencies, and other functionaries of mainstream offices and programs in the central city.

The country was stunned by the magnitude of what had transpired and became more so when, during the next four years, similar community explosions ripped at the guts of the many cities in which poor Blacks had become confined. No aspect of the Watts rebellion polarized Blacks and whites more than did the movement into the streets of hundreds of young Blacks, venting their wrath against confinement and closed opportunity; for as they left the Stronghold in Watts or wherever they were restricted in other cities, they became frighteningly visible to mainstream America. No longer statistics or abstract social profiles, they were animated, real people, a definite threat to peace, tranquility, and business as usual. Their visibility forced out into the open that reality which had for so long been denied —the separated existence of a growing underclass, hidden away in poverty-ridden enclaves in almost every city, blocked out of the daily sight of whites.

The mainstream reacted in a variety of ways. The official posture of the Establishment was expressed in Governor Brown's policy of containment—the sealing off of most of south Los Angeles through curfew imposition. More broadly, many white Americans responded by counting the cost of money and property lost. They could not comprehend how American citizens could unleash such a violent attack on the businesses and law enforcement personnel that presumably served them. How could anyone set fire to his own community? They failed to see that what the underclass men destroyed was precisely those buildings and businesses that were *not* their "own." The action was also incomprehensible to whites because they would never understand the depth of resentment harbored by young Blacks, who intuitively knew that much of their failure and underclass status derived from being Black in a racist-controlled, white society. Some few whites felt guilty but a much greater number were afraid and angry about what they had been forced to see. As a result, they sought to deny, to justify, and to further contain. Many tried to limit the importance of the upheaval or to view it as a conspiracy or justify the actions of the police. Most importantly, however, the rebellion forced both national and local governments to place on their agendas discussion of new policies and programs with respect to the future of Blacks in America.

The consequences for and the reactions of Blacks were equally complex. For Black America as a whole, the rebellion provided both relief and some embarrassment. The Watts youth had made a statement before the nation that others had tried to make diplomatically, but one that had gone unheeded. Some Blacks felt relieved; although they were unable to use the same methods the Watts youth had, they surely felt some satisfaction that a way had been found to bring the nation's attention to the plight of Blacks in the inner cities. Others were embarrassed and felt it necessary to apologize for the actions of Black youth who had gone on a rampage and who, in doing so, broke up the traditional charade of race relations. For the people of Watts, the aftermath brought relief from the bedlam of burning and seizure while it set the stage for a totally new drama that unfolded over the next ten years.

As daybreak came on the day following the official ending of the riot, the center of Watts had already been dubbed "Charcoal Alley." The streets were littered with debris, the air was acrid with the smell of smoke, and small groups of people huddled together to begin assessing the events of the past few days and nights. The explosion had created a new interest in the community among the residents, particularly those who had formerly been most alienated. The Parking Lot men spoke of having "immobilized" the Establishment, but far more significant was the fact that these former "unreachables" had established communication with the rest of Watts. Only a short time earlier their world had been no larger than the Parking Lot. But through their actions they had won the chance for a new dialogue with a broad cross-section—middle-income people, professionals, and business proprietors—of Watts. They valued their involvement not as a few days of revelry but as an experience worth exploiting—as a means to change. Other Blacks had also become more expansive and open to this contact as they realized that Watts symbolized a national condition. The new sense of Black unity was recalled by one young man this way:

> Everybody was sticking together. Everyone was calling each other "Brother." People were more civil, and there were no more fights between the brothers. Everyone spoke to each other.

Equally important, the men felt they had contributed to breaking the invisibility that had so long isolated them, as well as the ghetto. Ghettoization is confinement and obscurity. (What occurs inside a ghetto is more often than not maintained as news within the ghetto.) Those outside are insulated from the suffering, and often mayhem, which in fact occurs daily inside. Thus, one of the nearly universal conclusions concerning the explosion was that it had brought about greater awareness of the condition of Blacks:

The riots have caused everyone to wake up—in Watts and the outside world. For the first time they looked at the ghetto as it was.

It caused the whole world to wake. It stopped police brutality; this is what started it. It stopped the police from jacking you up all the time. Didn't burn nothing but junk anyway.

The men felt they had not only jolted Watts into becoming more aware of itself and its potential but had forced white society to recognize them:

We "made them" respond to our condition.

And contrary to the view of the broader community, the rebels were all proud they had become so visible. They saw this new state as a prelude to change, and yet they realized distinctly that improvement would not be possible without mainstream recognition of themselves and their condition.

Nearly all the men believed, too, that relations between Watts and the broader community had changed as a result of the new recognition. The residents of Watts seemingly had more power, at least a greater potential for commanding a hearing and a response from the white world. One source of this increased leverage was the fear aroused by the rebellion:

Yes, it [the rebellion] increased the feeling of power. It put fear on them patties; they're scared. The only ones you give respect to are those you fear.

The consensus was that a dialogue would soon begin between the people of Watts and the "people downtown." Without knowing either the agenda or the scope of the pending exchanges, they felt hopeful that a different kind of communication would occur, for any change would have to be an improvement over what had existed before. One activist noted:

It [the rebellion] couldn't set it [Watts] back any more than before, or we'd all be outside the door. What's to come—don't know, but it's here, man, they want to talk peace.

Here the feeling of unsureness remains, but the idea that any communication would just naturally be a change for the better predominates.

Despite some variations in their attitudes regarding the explosion's effect on the community of Blacks, almost every one of these men believed deeply that it had not set the community back because it had to come: dramatizing the condition of Blacks before the nation was necessary and good. Nevertheless, a small yet perceptive minority of these men continually warned against too much excitement over the prospect of positive changes. Their contention that the four-day upheaval had actually set up the community for reprisal was based primarily on their suspicion that Watts would be punished; it was under an unspoken obligation to do penance. As support for their view, they cited what they perceived as the beginning signs of this punishment, particularly the lack of repair or replacement of destroyed facilities. One pertinent comment was:

> Like I said, it made people afraid, and we can't have no good stores, nor no good food.

Still another reflected:

> Yes, it set us back, because the people will have to apologize after the event. How long it will last before it comes back to normal—actually it was never normal—I don't know.

As time passed, the men became increasingly uncertain about what they had accomplished. Although they believed the intensity of the explosion and its implied demands could not help but bring about some change in the white community's attitudes, the direction of that change was not at all clear. Would the fear they had provoked in a large section of whites cause an angry, resistive backlash, or would it force the various government officials and politicians to respond as a condition of peace?

Yet, aware of the divisions prevailing in the mainstream, the men were cautious about what they heard emanating from this sector. Even as communication was opening, many believed they were not receiving the full unadulterated message from the broader society, which was suspected of withholding its true reactions for fear of reigniting the rebellion or of seemingly giving too many concessions:

> Yes, the riot brought about more respect, to a certain extent . . . but they can't show it.

Strategies for the Future: Black Unity or Disunity?

It was in this no man's land, a new political arena where they had no precedents to draw upon, that these men found themselves post-rebellion, 1965. It was against this background that they had to make decisions about their future strategies. As they began to evaluate the situation, they came up against the issue of Blacks' operational unity, which the rebellion had pushed to the surface. Identifying and talking about "them" turned out to be much easier than defining "us." Despite the upsurge of community awareness and the sense of Black unity that occurred in the days following the explosion, deep splits remained between various interest groups. The unemployed and unskilled poor, the skilled unemployed, the moderate-income wage earners, the middle-income professionals and technicians, and the large numbers of steady low-income workers of Watts—all differed on some points. Even members of the Black intelligentsia were divided over their commitment to Blacks' independent development. A further division existed between the younger generation, as represented by the street rebels—the newly visible group that wanted to articulate the meaning of the explosion to society—and the older generation. And, in the end, there were sharp programmatic differences between the many newly emerged indigenous community groups. The young men of the Parking Lot believed that the community's new-found power, however much of it there might be, should be wielded primarily by the young, because they would not, presumably, have apologetic feelings about the community's rebellion and would therefore not become confused in negotiation with mainstream representatives. A typical expression of their attitudes toward their elders was this:

> The older people still talk critical, but they live in a dead life. They call us "dope heads," but they don't know what's happening.

Obviously, dialogues would have to occur among Blacks themselves before any meaningful exchange could begin with mainstream representatives. What was not clear was which section of Blacks would orchestrate these dialogues, who would be the participants—the representatives of the different interest groups—and how a position could be developed that would represent the whole community and still leave room for some specialized views to find expression. And after those questions were answered, who would articulate the programmatic need of Watts to the representatives of the broader society? Who would be the negotiators for Watts?

Underclass and Middle-Class Relations. Underlying much of the persistent conflict between the different sections of Blacks, particularly between the poor and younger street brothers and the achievers, was the matter of orientation—the beliefs and values that directed their life pursuits. As indicated at the end of the preceding chapter, underclass young men were critical of middle-income Blacks, citing their overcommitment to broader community concerns and their denial of any significant identification with or involvement in deep-seated problems of ghetto life. The young men saw their own identity and future primarily bound up with this confined community, whereas they believed that the middle-income Black saw his future largely in terms of the operations of mainstream society.

In spite of these criticisms of their middle-class brothers, the underclass men admired and respected them, too. Because their feelings about the achievers were so ambivalent—one moment based on their resentment of having been abandoned, the next based on an appreciation of their accomplishments—the youths' assessment of their kin shifted back and forth. On the one hand, it was clear to ghetto youth that middle-income Blacks are as much limited by racism as other Blacks and attain only those roles that the broader society makes available. Recognizing this severe limitation, they acclaimed the achievements of those Blacks who were deemed to have "beat the man's machine." One noted:

> He [the middle-class brother] must have something out there to beat whitey; otherwise, you know the man ain't going to use him.

They were proud of and deferential toward the striving Blacks' ability to succeed in the face of all the obstacles raised by society.

However, the ghetto-bound youth also asserted that the middle-income achiever "ain't doing shit, just running the high-sign on his brothers." This view came in part from two major beliefs. One, is the belief that no Black can obtain position in white society, even though he may demonstrate the exceptional skills needed to fill that position, unless the "man" wants him to. Therefore, since it is the mainstream that determines which jobs are made available, the ones offered to Blacks must be less valuable or, at best, second-level positions. Furthermore, they believe that the Black achiever, even when admitted to a high-status job, is not permitted to wield the full authority or perform all the functions commensurate with the position. Thus follows a third belief: that the achieving brother, aware of his underutilized capacity and second-class status even within the middle class, compensates for that status by parading insidious symbols of achievement before the underclass.

Another infrequently articulated paradox in this relationship was that while underclass Blacks criticized the middle class for its· mainstream orientation, they themselves held the commodity-consumption outlook and values of the broader society. In this respect, the aspirations of the two groups were not so distinctly different. What separated them chiefly was the underclass youths' lack of opportunity to gain access to paths of advancement in mainstream society. Their continued resistance to mainstream evaluations of their readiness or acceptability was due in large measure to their having been repeatedly denied opportunity in broader society and also due to the mainstream's repeated low evaluation of them. The underclass young men sought a context for striving and evaluation controlled by Blacks, thereby hoping to neutralize the experience of repeated failure and second-classness. Without knowing exactly how to solve the problem or what should constitute components for building such a model, they nevertheless felt that some form of collective Black community-based effort was necessary if a realistic solution were to be found. They felt that the successful operation of such a model would provide them with the ability to function on a socioeconomic par with people in the mainstream whether or not they selected broader society or Black society as their major context of social activity. Their conflict lay in their inability to develop and put into action such a model by themselves and therefore having to rely on the Black intelligentsia and professionals, who they doubted would assume this ethnic responsibility. Worst of all, in the end, even if such a commitment were undertaken, it would be no easy matter to develop a successful model controlled by Blacks; they suspected the "man" would institute new "games" to destroy any unified actions of Blacks.

The more the poor Blacks became entrenched, locked in the system of downward mobility, the more perceptive they became about the factors that impinge on their advancement and the more openly they expressed the belief that "whitey's" plan is to prohibit any significant alteration in their plight. There was seemingly less clarity or agreement about the methods necessary or available to oppose that plan. But they did tend to agree on one thing: They wanted to change the practices governing achievement rather than continue to attempt to meet present criteria as unfavored competitors.

Where Do We Go from Here? In the end, then, the men of the Parking Lot had to become more self-reliant. They knew they could receive only limited help from the Black achievers. They also knew their political entry into the arena of Watts might result in failure. They remained unsure about mainstream intentions and were doubtful of the role of Black intelligentsia. Nonetheless, they sought by their own means to overcome the problems of striving in a highly sophisticated racist society. They were not prepared either to return to the limited world of the Parking Lot or to sit as audience while the professional and income-earning Blacks negotiated a settlement. Neither were they of a mind to move aside, yielding to the many indigenous groups that began to emerge and articulate positions concerning the predicament of Watts. Strangely, these young men who had formerly been the most dissociated now demanded a voice as advocates for the poor population of Watts. And, what was probably most significant, they adopted the ghetto as the context within which to seek mobility and viable roles by developing self-help programs to accomplish these goals. Thus, still unemployed, unskilled, and poor, they had the audacity to try to create a self-help model for social development and to provide leadership for the community's redevelopment.

8

Participation in Community Change

The milieu in which the men of the Parking Lot had to make their way after the rebellion was a complex one, for Watts had become a laboratory for social experimentation on a scale never seen before in this or any other Black community. It was estimated that about one hundred new organizations were formed in less than a year. In addition to the programs developed and run by extra-ghetto agencies—the federal government's War on Poverty projects, unemployment services, special training efforts such as Youth Training Employment Programs, and experimental welfare programs such as Creating Neighborhood Day-Care Mothers—many local groups were created or revitalized. The standard political parties were stimulated to new activity, and this gave rise to a host of new community-based political groups. And such local organizations as the Westminister Neighborhood Association, the Watts Labor Action Council, the Green Power Movement, US, and the Young Men for Total Democracy became active forces as well. Even professionally based programs which resulted in the Central City Mental Health Clinic, the Watts Multi-Purpose Health Center, and activities of the National Association of Black Social Workers be-

125

gan to have an impact. Clearly, the unified voice of Watts that some had hoped for was slow in developing, but these various groups, with their own perspectives and goals, sought to bring about positive changes in the ensuing years.

Forming the Organization

A significant element in this scene was the Sons of Watts Improvement Association (SWIA). The development of this organization was slow and at times seemed almost impossible, but thanks to the perseverance of a handful of Parking Lotters and the dedication of Billy J. Tidwell, social work consultant to Watts community youth programs, the SWIA became a functioning entity in the political and economic quagmire of Watts.

Understandably, many of the men who had gained visibility during the Watts Rebellion had no wish to return to the obscure life of the Parking Lot, knowing that they would fare no better as individuals post-rebellion than they had pre-rebellion. They had no clout beyond the threat of potential explosiveness, and after the rebellion, even more than before, they were vulnerable to all the hardships of ghetto life. They had learned a lesson from the rebellion—ghetto individuals have little power to either attract attention or bring about change except when they combine their numbers and take action as a group. Thus, when eight young men informally decided to monitor and attend various community meetings concerned with the redevelopment of Watts, the stage was set for the emergence of the Sons of Watts.

Formal organization of the Sons was precipitated primarily by a community request for the Parking Lotters to participate in the First Watts Festival, which took place in August 1966 to commemorate the first Watts rebellion. The idea of holding the Festival grew out of concern—both within and outside the community—that the summer of 1966 would result in another explosion; despite the influx of so many new antipoverty programs, there had been no significant change in the socioeconomic condition of the Watts poor since the rebellion of August 1965. Although some Watts residents became connected with one or more poverty programs and others secured some limited income in experimental job programs, the majority remained untouched by these activities. In addition, and even more serious, their despair and restlessness increased as they witnessed mainstream reports of important social and economic change occurring in Watts—when in reality no such thing was happening.

As the summer of 1966 began, a group of business own-ers, residents, service organizations, and many others with Watts-based interests joined to organize the festival under the official sponsorship of the Jordan Downs High School Alumni. This group sought the support of the community for their plans. As part of that effort, they invited the men of the Parking Lot to serve as security forces for the festival. Gaining the support of the Parking Lotters, however, proved no easy matter. Many feared attachment with formal causes, as it would impose some controls on their activity and behavior; above all, it magnified their self-doubts about performing positive social roles ade-quately.

In the end, a small group of Parking Lotters accepted the invitation to participate and chose to be identified as the Sons of Watts. Over 35,000 people came to Watts for the festival; no major confrontations between participants or visitors occurred. Indeed, the festival proved so successful that it has become an annual event. At the conclusion of the 1966 festival, the young street men felt their activities were a success and had contrib-uted to the positive responses of the people. This experience mobilized their interests, leading them to consider deeper and more involved social roles, as the following quotations demon-strate:

> The thing that got me was the role I played in main-taining order in our own community. I became dedicated, as I saw everyone saying, "Welcome to Watts." No one was ashamed [of the rebellion]—they were proud. It made me proud of myself, especially to my brothers and sisters.

> I saw the power we had during the festival and the people's respect for us. When I decided to come [to the festival], at first I saw it as a good game. Then we talked about the Sons of Watts; it sounded like it could be some-

thing. Then I became a Sons of Watts. It's a good thing.
Let me tell you, we are a group of unique people; had
a chance of being the world's greatest pimps and gang-
sters. We acted bad; now we can be respected. We burned
four million dollars worth of property; we have power
and should be respected. We're trying to do something
different now.

Thus, moved by their recent accomplishments and motivated by the renewed hope attained through a better interaction
with the people of the community, a group of thirty young men
committed themselves in varying degrees to a totally new experience—possibly a new chance to live and to be. They became the
core of the Sons of Watts. Other Parking Lotters joined the Sons
tentatively, maintaining a peripheral and watchful association.
Although they were inclined to try the SWIA program, they remained skeptical. This tenuous connection was described by
one of the hard-core men who later joined the Sons:

> The rest of the fellows went out for this game—
> especially for the festival. I didn't go right then. Some-
> times I was a Sons of Watts and sometimes not. I dig
> what the fellows are trying to do, but like at first I didn't
> dig what they were doing. Now I feel the Sons of Watts
> will help not just me, but all the fellows. It can get jobs;
> give us something to do. . . . If the Sons make it, we make
> it, 'cause we're the Sons.

Still others were unable to make the necessary personal
commitment. Although they were truly impressed by what they
saw and even sought some loose association with the Sons, their
personal needs and commitments to a different life-style prevented uncompromised attachment. One of the young men who
was always at the periphery of the Sons activity noted:

> I don't know if I'm in or not. Maybe I'm not in it.
> I do what I want to do, 'cause my time ain't that much.
> The Sons are out there picking up garbage, fixing furni-
> ture. I stay out. I got to go places and do things. See, if

> I'm one [of the Sons], then I can't drink! They are righteous in outlook. They treat me like anybody else. For me there's nothing. I'm just me. They accept me. They're righteous, taking care of business. I still like to drink.

A few were even openly antagonistic, at least to start with. One of the men who held out said:

> At first I didn't buy it. Then I talked to two brothers who had become members of the Sons. They were for real. Before this, I was down on the Sons and even jumped a few; then I found out they were for real.

The SWIA's membership and organizational structure evolved slowly and informally. Movement in and out of the group was more common than steadfast commitment for most members in the early stages. Concessions in programs and policies were not uncommon in order to attract new members. In the first six months of the organization's life, there was a core group of leaders, but none had specific titles. Elections of officers developed much later.

Finding a Home. In spite of the reservations of some of the former rebels, the core group forged ahead. Once the Sons had established their presence and were legally incorporated (with the help of a social worker), the next step was to find headquarters. They hoped this new facility would not be too far from the traditional turf, the Parking Lot, and would be on 103rd Street, "where the 'action' was." These young men were not about to be removed from the center of community happenings. When they made their needs known, the community responded positively. Office space, a desk, office supplies, and telephones were made available to the new organization by a local press, the *Star Review.* This space, with its large glass window fronting on 103rd Street, became the executive office and the location of formal meetings. A second facility, acquired later, turned out to have an even greater effect on future developments. This abandoned gas station, located directly across from the Parking Lot and the Jordan Downs Housing Project, was rented through grant funding (from an absentee landlord) and designated the "Workshop." It was repaneled, painted, and furnished with odd pieces of furniture collected in the community. The Workshop served not only as a place to work, as its name implies, but as the main congregation spot for the majority of the members. Here, too, the members maintained their ties with those young men who were not yet ready to make the change from the Parking Lot to the Sons.

Defining the Purpose. The second task of the Sons was to develop a comprehensive statement of purpose. The ultimate goal, though never really formalized, emerged over a period of time: to increase the dignity of the people of Watts and their pride in their community. In working toward this end, the SWIA announced that they would engage in social actions directed at community improvement. Such self-help efforts were obviously needed, since it was clear that the city government and mainstream businesses were not interested in rebuilding Watts. After the explosion, the Sanitation Department had done just enough to remove major obstacles from the streets. And a year later the community still resembled a city bombed during a war. Plaster and rubble from burned-out buildings lay piled in vacant lots. Many storefronts had boarded windows, and there was no major-chain supermarket. In addition, electric lighting remained minimal, and construction was almost nonexistent. These conditions were the price they were paying for the rebellion. The rage that had motivated many of these young men to burn a section of this community was once again being rekindled, as they began to feel that Watts was never going to be rebuilt through outside community resources. This time, however, the young men tried to direct their anger toward constructive action.

Social Action Program

The initial programs of the Sons were intended to improve the image of the community. These activities were extremely important, because they required absolutely no help or sanction from the broader society.

Cleanup. As one of their very first efforts, the Sons se-cured some 100 old oil drums, which were converted into trash cans by cleaning and painting. Then the young men borrowed a truck from a local merchant and distributed these brightly painted cans with the name "Sons of Watts" inscribed on the sides. The cans not only discouraged littering but provided much publicity for the emerging organization. And the refurb-ishing and distribution of these drums provided productive, community-oriented activities for some thirty to forty men who for years had not been involved in any such positive community improvement effort.

The response of the community to this project made it almost immediately successful. Men and women, as well as youngsters, could be seen making that special effort to drop cigarette and candy papers into the Sons' trash cans.

Almost every store on 103rd Street had a can in front, and a number of owners who did not have them requested them. In fact, the response was so positive that it resulted in a problem of collection. The Sons negotiated with the Sanitation Depart-ment but failed to get help. Nevertheless, the Sons continued this service, collecting trash whenever the cans became full.

Publicity. A desire for greater visibility and action under-pinned considerations of future programs. The Sons had tasted acclaim, and they wanted more. Even when they congregated in front of their new headquarters, displaying their usual spirited communication style, they were no longer a symbol of fear to the people. The residents openly acknowledged them; The Sons, in turn, sought to maintain the community's confidence by dis-playing more respectful behavior. In their desire to be recog-nized, they had the "Sons of Watts" inscribed on a poster out-side the office's front window, on their car doors, and on bright red satin jackets. Now, these hitherto scorned young men of the Stronghold showed their increased sense of worth and pride as they walked up and down the streets, being greeted by and greeting men, women, and children from all walks of life.

Security Patrol. The next major Sons project was intended to rebuild the confidence of business owners and encourage po-tential community investors. Drawing on the idea of the contro-

versial but famed Community Alert Patrol, they established the
Sons of Watts Security Patrol, a free service whose purpose was
to directly safeguard business property when the owner requested protection. The SWIA hoped that this patrol would
"encourage burned-out businesses to return to the area and re-
duce exorbitant insurance rates. The most demoralizing and
conspicuous sights in Watts are the vacant lots, upon which used
to stand business establishments. . . . The SWIA, recognizing
that the lack of physical reconstruction and the maintenance of
protective measures are due to fear and insecurity, has seen fit
to provide the security themselves" (Tidwell, 1966, p. 3).

In a few old beat-up cars, with gas paid for from a small
treasury already being built up by the Sons' organization, the
Patrol took to the streets. Three or four men officially armed
with nothing more than flashlights and their sense of "right"
manned these autos—clearly marked "Sons of Watts Security
Patrol"—throughout the night until the early hours before daybreak. Each morning a group of weary young men could be seen
returning to the Workshop pleased and proud that they had put
in their time.

They even managed to fulfill these responsibilities without abandoning certain aspects of their basic life-style. For instance, one member spoke of how on the previous night they
had encountered a young lady in the course of their patrol; and
as social custom dictated, an exchange ensued—resulting in
a new relationship. "She was great, baby, but I was on patrol,
so I'm going to see that action today." As all the Sons understood, "You have to take care of business."

These highly activist young men gradually expanded the
functions of the Patrol. Assisted by a walkie-talkie, they began
to cruise around, prepared to dissuade or apprehend persons
they thought had violated a peaceful atmosphere or had injured
others. No longer were the patrol members only protecting specific events or businesses at night. And the excitement and quasi-
legitimate (without official police sanction) exercise of authority
served to stimulate many of the less organizationally oriented
Parking Lotters to participate in the Sons' development.

Working with Children. Their increased visibility in community-sanctioned social roles led the Sons to undertake less dramatic but nonetheless important programs to help the children of Watts. The impetus for the safety program was the perceived problem of unsupervised crosswalks and too few crossing guards. "In Watts one all too frequently hears of accidents involving children going to and coming from school. Many such accidents have been due to deficient supervision at strategic intersections and crosswalks. The SWIA, in an expression of concern for the welfare of Watts children, will offer its assistance and manpower to preserve their safety" (Tidwell, 1966, p. 3).

As a result, some of those men who only a short time before had been viewed as "school dropouts" and therefore as outcasts could now be found supervising the crosswalks of three elementary schools. This demonstration of concern and the contacts the Sons made with the children and teenagers of the community resulted in new communication. Some of the youngsters saw their older brothers performing a socially useful function for the first time instead of smoking dope on the Lot. And there was much joking and jibing as the children saw former hustlers intently halting traffic as they crossed the streets.

These contracts were the stepping-stones to a counseling relationship. The Sons, many of whom had extensive histories of delinquent and antisocial behavior, contemplated a program in which they would become positive role models for the younger boys and girls. As counselors, they would try to modify the adolescents' dysfunctional behavior and decrease the number of school dropouts. The statement supplied by the SWIA noted that:

> Experience is the best teacher, and it takes one who has experience to counsel another. Virtually all of the SWIA members have experienced difficulties with law enforcement and school personnel. By virtue of these experiences, they are well suited to advising youngsters who are in danger of making the same mistakes. Furthermore, they have been revered and identified with by these youngsters. The role model which the Sons of Watts

portray now, however, is completely antithetical to that which they displayed prior to organizing. It is expected that young potential and confirmed delinquents in the area will be as compelled to identify with this new model as they were with the old [Tidwell, 1966, p. 3].

Even before the program was officially implemented, many informal counseling relationships had already been established. For instance, Sons could be seen leaving the Parking Lot and driving to a crowd of some forty to fifty youngsters surrounding an after-school fight. They would enter the youthful crowd, separate the youngsters, and engage them in discussion, while others "cooled out" the agitators. They would emphasize the destructiveness of young Black children fighting among themselves and the poor image it created in the community. The response of the youngsters was phenomenal. They would stop and attempt to use the Sons as moderators in their battle. The shift by the youngsters from an emphasis on gaining a "rep" to an emphasis on moderating their differences became a significant new dynamic in the young street life of 103rd Street.

Yet the Sons did not forget their old patterns of behavior. They not only remembered but often recalled with some enthusiasm their street rumbles and how they attained their "rep." Many still manifested much of the energy and restlessness that poverty life provokes. Thus drawing on their previous knowledge (and from their ranks, a former boxer), they instituted a boxing program for the youth in the community. Although there was no regular schedule, anyone driving by the Jordan Downs Project on any given day could probably have found a large crowd of young men and adolescents "putting up their dukes" under the watchful eye of the former professional boxer, who had suffered an ignominiously shortened career when his license was revoked following an encounter with police. But rather than anger and hostile "signifying," there was the festive spirit of young men in open sports competition.

This program was crude, lacking not only regular scheduling but adequate facilities. The Parking Lot and occasionally the gym in the Jordan Downs Project were used in place of a community center. Instruction was irregular because the instructor still had to spend much of his time seeking out odd jobs for income. The lack of a community center with an adequate ring, paddings, and other equipment resulted in some minor cuts and bruised shoulders, but the program continued undaunted.

The new contact with the younger teens of Watts opened other avenues too. For example, the Sons painted and cleaned up the Workshop—which was usually filled with tools, unfinished furniture, wood shavings, and beer cans—in preparation for an after-school "Philly-Dog" and "Skate" dance program. The furniture, remodeled by the Sons, now decoratively lined the walls. Burlap drapes strung over a large wire gate provided privacy and a clublike atmosphere. One of the Sons was at the entrance to the Workshop. It was now approaching 4 P.M.; he had worked off his earlier buzz, had gone home, had put on his ascot, and was now collecting quarters from all those who entered. The phonograph loudly played "Just Call on Me," as the boys and girls—heads bobbing and all—worked out.

Christmas Special. The Sons refused to accept the community's being poorly lighted or undecorated as the Christmas season approached. They were determined to provide an exciting holiday for the children of Watts. Angels cut out of wood and colored with bright paint and luminescent speckling were made for the main section of 103rd Street. Christmas lights were obtained for the streets, toys were solicited from various agencies, and one of the Sons was chosen to be Santa Claus.

Much effort went into preparation in the last few days before Christmas. The Sons decorated the Workshop, and by Christmas Eve the lights went on in Watts. Decorations hung from the city electric poles. The children massed around the Santa, eagerly clutching the toys he gave out. Songs of the season rang out, and for a few fleeting days the spirit of Peace on Earth and Good Will Toward Men reigned. This spirit was short-lived for the children, since seven days after Christmas they watched their Santa Claus being busted by the "black and white" for alleged narcotics use. No evidence secured, no official charge brought against Santa Claus, just the smashed dreams for the children of Watts.

A Broader Scope

Through these various activities the Sons increasingly emerged as a potent social force within the community. They had made the residents aware of their power and influence. They were no longer a group of displaced young men making some big claims about community improvement but a more polished, confident, and proud organization. Recognition of their new pride and power was granted not only by local residents but by various representatives of the broader community. Within Watts, various agencies consulted them about community problems. Residents stopped in the offices of the Sons seeking guidance on family and personal matters. And social-action groups sought support for united community endeavors. In the white community important recognition came from the news media—the press, radio, and television—who sought the opinions of the Sons on various newsworthy events. In addition, Los Angeles County agency representatives consulted with the Sons; the Human Relations Commission opened up an informal dialogue; persons representing outside businesses, including building and contracting concerns, sought the Sons' approval for their community-based activities; and numerous individuals of significance in the political, social, and economic life of the broader community sought to open up a dialogue with the Sons.

Let There Be Light. On the basis of this newly accorded importance, the SWIA tried to gain concessions from agencies of the broader community that would improve Watts. One attempt was to increase street lighting, which, as indicated earlier, was particularly inadequate in contrast to that of neighboring municipalities. Only during the Watts Festival had there been enough lights to illuminate the streets. In their early Statement of Goals, the Sons noted:

> It is a long-standing sociological fact that darkness is more conducive to criminal activity than is daylight.

However, even with this knowledge, Watts (alleged to have one of the highest delinquency and crime rates in the city) is without sufficient street lighting in many sections of the community. The SWIA, heretofore delinquents and criminals themselves, have determined to rectify this condition.

This project was a new experience for the members of the young organization. They were now dealing not with their own community but with mainstream-controlled bureaucracy, from whom they wanted to obtain changes in policy. They first had to learn which organization to contact and then how to handle the encounter. When the Department of Water and Power became the target, further questions arose. Should the Sons go down to the department's offices, and if so, how many? With whom should they ask to speak? And finally, irrespective of the importance and justifiability of their request, whom did the Sons represent? Was theirs a request or a demand?

The Sons finally made contact, but to no avail. The streets remained poorly lighted. Much anger and frustration arose again in the members. They could only assume the resistance by those in power to correcting the Watts lighting condition must stem from the fact that the request came from Watts. (This was only another way of saying a Black community.) The irony of the situation—former criminals trying and failing to correct a condition conducive to criminality—did not escape them either.

New Political Roles. On September 28, 1966, the news broke that in the sister city of San Francisco, in the ghetto of Hunters Point, the young residents were in an open confrontation with the police and officials of the city. The young Blacks, suffering from many of the same conditions that had existed in Watts threatened to duplicate the events in Southern California. The Sons listened to the radio and scanned the papers continually as they followed developments. The phones in their offices rang incessantly, as news columnists, government officials, and members of social movements wanted to get their reaction to the crisis.

Finally, Hunters Point exploded, and, as in Watts, the anger of Black ghetto dwellers was released. On the third day of the outburst, the SWIA issued an official statement. Although much heated discussion had taken place among the members, who felt great sympathy for the young men of Hunters Point, the statement of the SWIA, heard throughout the nation on television, said "Cool it, brothers, you have made your point." This statement was significant, as it expressed officially a shift away from their earlier unofficial posture of unequivocal alliance with ghetto rebellions. Though it represented an attempt to remain identified and allied with the ghetto brothers in their demands, it also repudiated violence as a way to correct conditions of poverty and injustice.

This statement also revealed the more complex political role of the Sons. As public recognition came to the organization, more and more official persons wanted statements, opinions, and suggestions not just about simple local problems but about wider issues. The Sons were now being called upon to take sides, to differentiate their positions from those of other agencies and movements. They were beginning to be asked which commissioner of police they preferred, whether they would support Stokely Carmichael's community appearance, and many other questions whose answers had broad implications and, most of all, required a political posture.

One issue on which they took sides had especially strong repercussions. In October 1966, the Sons decided to picket the local Workers International Bookstore. This action was undertaken after the word had been received by the Sons, allegedly from the sheriff's deparment, that a local "communist group" was distributing literature that urged the youth of Watts to be openly militant in their protests against police activity. The wording and the content were deemed inflammatory. The decision to picket was made to protest the dissemination of literature that might stimulate young people to act rashly and thereby jeopardize their lives needlessly. A further and unstated purpose appeared to be a desire by certain members of the Sons to distinguish the SWIA program of militancy from other movements in the community.

The picketing was covered by national television and the press, which stated, "Negroes in poverty organize against the activities of the local communists." The responses from many areas within and outside of Watts were dramatic, the majority of the calls to headquarters being critical of this activity. The critics were not worried so much about the communists as about whether the Sons had "gotten into Charlie's bag," that is, joined the Establishment. The intensity of the reaction was felt particularly by the Sons' adviser, Billy J. Tidwell, who reported receiving threatening phone calls and expressed concern about the safety of his family. The Sons rebounded by unanimously mobilizing to support and protect their adviser.

These two actions—the responses to the Hunters Point riot and the picketing—raised a fundamental question: What was the most effective way for the SWIA to bring about change in the community? Should it continue as it was originally constituted, namely, as an organization that did not ally itself with the goals, practices, and orientations of the broader community, or would it be more successful if it could obtain support for its position from outside sources? The members were divided on this issue, and it was never really resolved. Their stance usually depended on what seemed appropriate at the moment. And thus the activities and direction of the movement continued to be diverse and highly dependent on external events.

The Sons Bury Their Own

Often actions and statements were provoked by an unplanned event in the harsh life of the community. One such was the death of a Black teenager. Over station KATV the newscaster announced that the night before the L.A.P.D. had apprehended two youths in a "stolen car," and when the officers approached the auto, one of the suspects was alleged to have moved his hand in a menacing way. Consequently, he was shot and killed.

I recall hearing the report on my car radio on the way to the Sons' office that morning. When I arrived, I realized there was something special in the day's air. The office was unusually crowded with young men, many looking stern, others offering only clipped greetings while they paced the floor. Through the snatches of grumbled conversation and swearing, the essential message was passed on to every new arrival: "They have killed another one of us." The street system of communication had earlier revealed that the dead teenager was an associate but an unsigned member of the Sons of Watts and was well known to the men from the Stronghold. Once they heard his age on the news reports, they contacted other teenagers and ascertained where he lived and with whom. The phone rang; it was station KGFJ wanting a statement from the Sons. The back room of the office was the area of decision making. Those present held a strategy meeting and decided to protest this action of the police. They issued a statement expressing their repugnance at the methods of the police and asking for an immediate hearing and sanctions against the officers involved.

Having made their official statement, they then shifted to the immediate business at hand—helping the family. They called the dead youth's mother, in the name of the SWIA, and offered condolences. The mother's response was that of a woman who had suffered long, quietly, and almost helplessly. She expressed her thanks for the Sons' concern and noted that no other group had contacted her in this time of need. She would be pleased to see a delegation of the Sons, for she was just sitting at home waiting to obtain the body of her son.

Several members went to the house and aided in the funeral arrangements. And later the Sons of Watts acted as pallbearers as well as a security patrol during the services. The police and sheriff's department were notably absent, by agreement with the Sons of Watts, as they buried a child of the community.

Programs for Personal Growth

The SWIA program of social action was not only directed at influencing community change but was also an effort to enhance the personal development of the individual members. Through members' involvement in responsible, community-based activity, the problem of long-term, obsolete social roles was attacked. In addition to changing the characteristic dysfunctional street behavior, special sensitivity sessions were created. A group encounter program, run by the Sons and known as "blow sessions," was combined with a formal group instruction program to teach more effective leadership skills and communication techniques and to help members acquire new methods of resolving problems. Social workers conducted the formal training sessions at the social agency—Special Services for Groups (SSG). Prior to agency meetings, briefing sessions were held in which the issue of the pending meeting was discussed and strategies and roles were developed and rehearsed. Regularly scheduled meetings with agency and SWIA program personnel gave the men an opportunity to learn about programs and the agency's working methods and goals. It was hoped that the combined opportunity to perform positive roles through community action and to be supported by psychoeducational group sessions would result in important behavioral and attitudinal changes, particularly in transforming some of the men's negative self-images and while providing alternatives to destructive activity.

Group Communication, Problem Solving, and Leadership. As noted earlier, the Workshop was not only a place of work but a social center—the forum of the Sons. In between work activities, or when there was no work, or even during projects, these young men talked about community problems and had to make realistic decisions for the future. These exchanges were different from the "just plain bullshit" of the street culture, which was a way of individual socialization; the men were now seriously involved and committed to finding solutions for group and community problems. But the need to adopt formal procedures for attaining consensus soon became apparent when the sixty to seventy participants were unable to move their policy discussions to a conclusion. The old methods of decision making, effective in the informal, fragmented groups on the Parking Lot, were no longer useful. Initially, debates would go on into the early morning hours, each hour plagued by some personal confrontation as the old ways of communication were resorted to. On more than one occasion, members were seriously injured during these sessions when patience wore thin and wine increased their readiness to fight.

The executive body took this problem under consideration and proposed a format in which business would be completed first, and then discussions of the more familiar, less-
structured type could take place. The first step involved lessons
in basic parliamentary procedures taught by social workers.
These procedures were modified or suspended on special occasions when the Sons voted to hold a "blow session." Such a session, augmented with food and drink, allowed all the members
to discuss, debate, and "blow on" all questions, using the forms
they were most comfortable with. Through repeated training,
the formal procedures were slowly incorporated in the business
meetings. However, the informal exchanges were still common.
The new factor in both situations was an almost total absti-
nence from physical confrontations between members. It became an accepted rule that all members had a right to participate and to have differing opinions, but they would not fight
among themselves.

Some of their difficulties in communicating and inclina-
tion to fight derived from the leadership split that developed as
the Sons grew. This split was in turn due partly to the earlier
gang alliances they had brought with them from the Parking Lot.
One group of leaders—the executives who worked in the storefront headquarters—represented Watts at various conferences,
were the most articulate members, and were, in terms of the
hustling typology presented earlier, the "players." These young
men, carrying attache cases and sometimes wearing suits and ties
(in style emulating the Madison Avenue image), had emerged as
the spokesmen for the Sons in the broader society.

The other leaders also held formal positions in the SWIA,
but their province was the Workshop. They were closer to the
Watts community currents and maintained daily and extensive
contact with the larger Sons' membership. They also sustained
the dialogue with those brothers who remained in the Stronghold. Their special competence was based on having had some
work experience, and they were primarily interested in activity.
The Workshop leaders obtained some support from a social
work agency, Special Services for Groups (funded by the Economic Youth Opportunity Agency from 1965 to 1968), which

as part of its "Escape String" project employed ten of them as consultants in a work-related program for poverty-area unemployed youth.

Although these two leadership groups appeared to have complementary skills and activities, the underlying conflict continued to build, exacerbated by the increased attention the SWIA received from local and mainstream factions and by the constant worry about money. Twice the conflict became so severe that special blow sessions had to be held. Here the members had the opportunity to air their suspicions, misgivings, and anxieties. These were found to be based on poor communication between the leaders and the rank and file and, to a lesser degree, on the "signifying" that took place among the members, many of whom still exhibited the intense paranoia necessary for Parking Lot survival rather than the trust needed in this new situation. Furthermore, the frustrations of nonachievement encouraged them to question the worth of investing in new social roles. Interestingly, on both occasions the crisis abated because the men were able to directly address the issues, and a stronger, more closely knit organization and leadership emerged.

These blow sessions, like others they had, resembled encounter group meetings. They became effective instruments for dealing openly with conflicts. Many of the members who had felt that their thoughts and suggestions were unimportant and who saw themselves as being unable to contribute articulately in the formal organizational setting gained immeasurably from these experiences. The sessions also increased the ability of the members to clearly express to outsiders what the Sons were all about. But probably the most vital result of these sessions was the somewhat less tangible feeling of respect and increased personal worth on the part of individual members. In these meetings the men talked of being Black, of how they experienced the "man," of the deep anger they carried, and of what they would have to do to change their life situation. The Brothers questioned and confronted one another, forcing each other to define platitudinous expressions. They hit hard, and if a man could not stand the heat, he had better learn how because they were going to "tell it like it is."

Training for Employment

Probably the Sons' single most important and long-lasting program was undertaken in the Workshop. Although many of the more publicized efforts were finalized in and launched from the Sons' headquarters, the Workshop was the center of information exchange and informal decision making. For the many unemployed young men, the day began and ended here. It operated officially from 9 A.M. to 10:30 P.M. but functioned unofficially twenty-four hours a day.

The main purpose of the training program was to help the members regain some identification and practice with work roles, because, as we have seen, many of the Sons had been unsteadily employed or unemployed for years owing to criminal records, job discrimination, early school termination, and ultimately psychological debilitation. This long isolation from the job market placed them in a position where they were unable to compete adequately with the more fortunate employed youth of Watts, much less with the favored competitors of white society. In addition, being isolated from formal Black society and its network or agency contacts such as the Urban League or a union like the Brotherhood of Sleeping Car Porters, increased the severity of their employment problems. To correct their obsolete condition, the programs taught them techniques for effective job application as well as provided them with some marketable skills. Member-to-member aid was an important element in the training procedure: Those who had work experience became teachers, practicing supervision and instruction while imparting their skills and knowledge to their brothers. Volunteers from the community provided further instruction. For those who had no previous training and who felt inadequate because of their obsolescence, being taught in a less structured, supportive environment, close to their brothers, was often conducive to learning.

The primary skill taught was furniture upholstering and repair. This was selected because knowledgeable teachers were available and because of its future utility: "Upholstering is a reasonably high-demand occupation. In that the wage scale for this type of work is attractive, in that several public schools have discontinued training in this field, and in that the SWIA has at least two members who are competent, skillful furniture repairmen, it is felt that an indigenous training program in this particular skill would be a valuable community service" (Tidwell, 1966, p. 1). Owing to limited tools and materials, and to uncertainty about the men's response, the program was begun on a limited basis with ten trainees. A few tools were obtained through donations. One piece of furniture in need of upholstering was secured from a community resident and repaired; payment was subsequently received for rebuilding it. The initial achievements attested to the plausibility of such a program.

Realizing that this training program produced only limited results, as it did not seriously affect the intense stagnation of many of the unemployed men, the SWIA undertook a job-development program in conjunction with the Management Council—a group of Los Angeles area business representatives that offered voluntary managerial help to fledgling enterprises and limited job placement services to the community. This endeavor was "designed to secure job placements for SWIA members particularly, and unemployed residents in general. Much consideration is being given to those individuals who have had difficulty in getting employment due to delinquent and/or criminal records" (Dunbar and others, 1967, p. 4). These program innovations ultimately had little effect on the core problem of unemployment, but the SWIA had tried to alter its members' economic obsolescence. If nothing else, it gave some members rudimentary salable skills and others their first experience with organized work despite such program handicaps as a dearth of supplies, inadequate equipment, and a lack of outside work opportunity.

Although most of the early Sons' programs were later terminated, particularly those directed at improving both the atmosphere of Watts and the citizens' attitudes toward the community, a few notable exceptions remained. One such program, initiated in 1967 to create jobs and provide vocational training, was the Sons of Watts Gas Station. This project was assisted by the Standard Oil Corporation, whose involvement was encouraged by representatives of the then Congressional District office of Agustus Hawkins. Standard Oil subsidized and provided credit and training to members of the Sons with the understanding that they would ultimately run an independent gas station. After moving from its original location of 103rd Street to 120th Street and Central Avenue, the gas station continued to sell gasoline and provide repair work for Watts commuters as late as 1975. One member of the Sons held primary responsibility for this program throughout the years.

Another successful long-term program—a Release on Own Recognizance (ROR) System was set up under the Model Cities Program in 1972. This program gave many ghetto residents an opportunity for release from imprisonment. In addition, it provided court counseling, post-release employment counseling, help with securing residences, and assistance in getting back to the courts for hearings. Members of the Sons served as agents and counselors in this program.

Impact on the Members

The total effect of the Sons of Watts on its members was most dramatic. In the two and a half years since these men had left the Parking Lot to demonstrate their anger against the system, they had experienced personal growth in varying ways. In identifying the factors that had influenced these changes, some spoke of the feeling of increased visibility and power they had obtained from belonging to the organization:

> Now I have constructive ideas, and through this organization I can put them into action. I am the Sons of Watts and therefore I can get something for the community.

For another, having a stable place was important:

> Yes, actually we don't hang around the Parking Lot. There's a place to come to if you don't have anything else. I've gained a little more respect for myself.

This young man gained confidence:

> It [the SWIA] has proven to me that I didn't have to be afraid. Now I can go for the bigger things

and not stay with the smaller things. I don't have to be afraid of the "man." Now I speak to him the way I want to. When you're paid, you have to listen. Now I can say what I want, even refuse, or negotiate if I want.

Others referred to obtaining meaningful roles in the organization's program as a contributing factor:

Everyone in the Sons of Watts is going to be helped. Everybody, not only me. I've learned a little bit from the Sons. . . . Instead of standing on the street and getting drunk, I now have some things to do.

Another saw it this way:

I don't do the things I used to do. I used to split when the police came around: Now I'm proud; I don't run no more. It helps my pride, and now lets us do something in the community; we're something today and respected.

And even one young man who had a reputation for vamping on women noted:

Yes, I've cut down on the "Hey, mama" shit, "I'd like to get into them drawers" stuff, and breaking wine bottles on the street. Now women come in the office and the Workshop; we're cleaning up the place. Now the place is nicer and open. This has helped me stop all that werewolf talking.

Other members specifically referred to psychological changes which had taken place. These men distinguished between the social roles performed and the new feelings derived from them:

To me it seems I feel better with myself and my community. I'm involved with the community now, not myself. For myself, I found out that I get along; people talk about you and now within myself I feel good. Now I uphold my Sons; no more fights like on the Parking

Lot; I show more respect for people and myself and the members of the organization.

There's a 100 percent difference. My personality has changed; plus I don't gamble no more—just drink on weekends. Before, I didn't care about shit. Now I take care of my wife and home, take home literature and read it with the family. We [the SWIA] receive letters offering help and encouragement. These encourage us. I've got it inside now. Maybe I got 10 percent left of those off-the-wall ways. The cops try to discourage us, but we just don't react.

Change and growth were not universal however. Some of the men, although they had had some new experiences in different social roles, continued to doubt the authenticity of all that was going on. They clung to their former behavior and orientation, measuring the changes cautiously and making only the most tenuous adjustments. One of these men, who exemplified the attitude of those who maintained a questioning skepticism, noted:

Things haven't really changed. I'm not working. I don't drink as much, no more fights, though most things are the same.

An eighteen-year-old who remained dubious about recent changes stated:

Things are slightly different. There are people who recognize the community needs and want to help, but still the outsiders come in to make a bone. The police continue to do the same job, as if you're an animal—nigger so and so—even with your wife and girlfriend. If there is any change, it will be due to orders from upstairs.

The feelings expressed by these men, although they were a minority, were important and should not be minimized, particularly because they represented the views of many others who maintained only peripheral associations with the Sons—those who typically hung out in the Parking Lot, skeptically observing the Sons' activities. They did not really think the Sons "game" would work, and even if it did, they did not know where they fit.

Conclusion

Without doubt, the Sons of Watts Improvement Association in its formative stages contributed importantly to bringing about changes in Watts and in many of its members. There were both successes and setbacks in pursuing the program goals of community betterment, but the overall effect was good. And the impact on the men of their experience as Sons was significantly greater than any measures of individual achievement would have revealed. Becoming acquainted with positive roles resulted in social and psychological growth, and they were able to attain a degree of social power through their membership in a formal organization. They regained at least a sense of belonging and in some cases even made notable contributions to the community.

Without denying the significance of these developments, however, one must acknowledge their limitations. When the real issues of productive functioning are examined, the most obvious fact is that these men continued to be jobless, poor, and occupationally obsolescent. Despite their efforts at self-help, no stable economic future was in sight. For the most part, the income-producing programs did not materialize, and although their job-hunting and market-analysis skills became a little more sophisticated, these improvements did not pay off in increased employment because the opportunity was not there. The self-help, community service-oriented programs, although very few, nevertheless continued to be the most lasting functional part of their activity. These at least provided jobs for some members and offered the community a service. Much of the early enthusiasm for the Sons had worn off by 1975. The equation of oppressive poverty had not been broken, and instead increasingly broken was the will of many of the men. Opportunities for a stable, income-producing job and avenues to upward mobility remained closed.

9

Reassessing the Issues

Ten years later, in 1975, nearly all these young men were back where they started from—an invisible part of the statistics of poverty, unemployment, and entrapment. When I asked about them on the streets of Watts that year, some of the new generation of youth could still recall the Sons of Watts, but fewer could point out where the organization had been located just a few years earlier. According to the reports, most of the Sons had moved—many south to Compton. Others were serving time. Four were said to have been killed. The only two recalled by names were thought to be "possibly into something," but they were no longer in Watts. One had left for northern California; the other was in the neighboring community of Compton.

In addition to the absence of the Sons, I saw other changes in Watts. For one thing, there were a number of new buildings whose signs indicated the development of a permanent social services network. These joined the Doctor Building and the Watts Health Foundation (formerly the Multi-Purpose Health Center), which had been established in the sixties. Murals depicting the Black life of Watts were painted on the walls of some of the new buildings. Notably missing, however, were the social activists flooding the streets and the many mobile offices set up in the sixties for emergency responses to the community's needs. In the mid seventies, the arenas of social protest had been relocated. Now they were found in the political caucuses; the

151

publications of small inner-city research firms, which pointed out the worsening condition of need among Blacks; and the papers delivered at conferences by Black educators, sociologists, social workers, psychologists, and other professionals who examined the special problems of those confined to the ghetto. Solutions were sought through trade-offs between different segments of society and through negotiated settlements.

But these latter changes serve only to emphasize the persistence of the underlying conditions. Because mainstream institutions continue to replicate the conditions experienced by the youth who rebelled in the sixties, a large portion of the young men of the seventies are becoming the new products of rejection, the occupationally obsolete. As school terminations and unemployment continue to increase, so do the ranks of those who had become the community's initial underclass members of the sixties.

Personal Deficiency and Alienation

Special populations of youthful poor have always existed in ghettos. These groups have traditionally been identified as different from white society, as well as from the larger community of Blacks. Supposedly, they formed a unique subculture characterized not only by significantly different attitudes and aspirations but by special exotic and deviant practices. Today, the young members of the Black underclass collecting in the inner cities are said to be part of this tradition, but they are represented in greater numbers and have greater visibility than ever before. In the sixties, as noted earlier, growing pockets of poverty in ghettos throughout the nation were attributed to poor nutrition, substandard housing, a lack of intellectual stimulation, and a constellation of related factors. Such poverty-ridden groups were considered culturally deprived and therefore unable to master mainstream educational paths or to meet the social demands of broader society.

The essentials of this theory continue to be applied, but now analysts stress the skills deficit side of the picture. Hence, in addition to being culturally deprived, underclass Blacks are now said to also lack the technological training and skills needed to meet labor market demands; thus they are condemned to perpetual unemployment and poverty. Again the blame for their condition is laid at their own doorstep. Both the culture of poverty theory and the skills deficit theory deny the societal factors that produce not only pockets of poverty but also widespread underclass growth and consolidation. The seemingly isolated poverty among young Blacks in the sixties was only an early stage of what has become widespread underclass entrapment.

Continuing to treat the symptoms rather than the causes of underclass development among Blacks is a useless effort; concentrating on treating individual Black youth for deficits rather than on correcting the structural factors that limit equal opportunity only perpetuates inadequate institutional services for ghetto populations and rehabilitative programs that do not create clear paths to real achievement for ghetto youth. Removing the dichotomy between mainstream-propagated expectations and limited available options could encourage large numbers of Black youth to successfully engage in realistic activity for achievement. But the poverty culture—lack of skills—argument is firmly backed by subtle mainstreamers' belief that Blacks' cultural, intellectual, and motivational inadequacies are the reasons for their large-scale underachievement.

A somewhat similar line of thinking was behind the solution proposed in the sixties to the widespread educational underachievement in the inner cities; that solution relied principally on school integration—requiring Black youth to attend schools with white youth in order to improve the Blacks' learning capacity—and subtly supported the belief that some sort of magic should happen to Blacks through their association with whites. Much more probable, however, is that any difference in achievement that occurred post-busing would be due to Blacks' having gained access to better school systems. Institutions with ample and experienced teaching faculty, greater range and supply of learning materials, and, in some cases, opportunity to participate in experimental learning environments (all benefits consistently lacking in one or another combination in ghetto schools) are likely to have greater impact than is the Black-white association. Thus it is not inconceivable that ghetto schools could become proficient institutions of learning with the proper apportionment of resources.

By reinforcing whites' belief in the inherent inadequacy of Blacks, the deficit skills theory subtly justifies for whites their continued receipt of preferential treatment: Since youthful Blacks are considered to have failed to achieve upward mobility because of their own incapability, they can without social guilt be legitimately banished to the wasteland of the ghetto. At the same time, many Black achievers are also made to feel distinctly different from the underachieving Blacks. They are encouraged to believe that exceptional individual capacity alone led to their success and that they thus need not identify too closely with the plight of the underclass. Although those who have achieved undoubtedly demonstrated exceptional capacity and energy, many equally capable Blacks have never achieved because they lack both the opportunity to choose from the full range of career options available to whites and the systemal support from those who control economic markets. The controllers traditionally provide preferential opportunity to members of their own ethnic, racial, religious, or primary interest group. In the absence of these two aids to achievement, many Blacks have been successful primarily through hard work, "stick-to-itiveness," and most important, chance—being at the door when entry is allowed.

Inevitably, Black achievers are still cited as proof that discrimination or structural barriers are not at the base of large-scale Black underachievement; Black middle-class success is widely trumpeted as testimony to the open character of American society. What has not even been addressed, however, is the second-class nature of Black middle-class status. Again, this is not because of personal inadequacy but because of the limited opportunities and functional roles made available to Blacks by broader society.

Alienation from mainstream values is another reason often given for the alleged differences between Black achievers and Black nonachievers who have failed to gain stable livelihoods. However, the present study finds that the bulk of inner-city young men, although somewhat resistant to adoption of main-stream social codes and behavior, nevertheless hold many of the same attitudes regarding consumerism, status symbols, and goals for attainment. Many continue to see the objects of their striv-ings as existing in broader society; and they hope that someday they will reach those goals. Yet, many of these youths maintain little, if any, faith in mainstream's intention to accord them equality; in fact, they view white society's institutions as a net-work organized to "do them in," to destroy them. Where the avenues to mainstream achievement are closed to them, under-class youth so often seek success within other available systems, sometimes in the illegitimate sector of the mainstream and other times in both the legitimate and deviant spheres of the Black community. Still others, with increasing frequency, withdraw from participation in either of these directions, choosing instead to gain livelihoods through hustling, welfare-connected programs, or other low-income or poverty programs.

Such detachment from broader society by underclass males is often viewed as representative of their inadequacies, but the failure of mainstream institutions to fully socialize Black youth to the mobility dream may have less to do with young Blacks' incapacity to absorb than with their resistance to pur-suing mainstream myths. In other words, their failure to be-lieve in the Horatio Alger proposition may speak to their social consciousness or their intuitive resistances rather than individual deficits or alienation. It is obvious that society must remove those structural and institutional barriers that have limited ac-cess in the past and must provide a broader range of opportun-ities to the underclass, as was attempted by the affirmative ac-tion programs of the sixties. These programs recognized the need for special action to remove the social impediments to Black achievement and represented in philosophy, if not always in practice, a national policy for changing the condition of Blacks that was both effective and realistic. The most important plank of this policy was the placement of Blacks in meaningful jobs and positions, thus providing access to opportunities heretofore prohibited by agency and institutional practices. Low-income Blacks responded to the new opportunities and demonstrated their capacity to learn, to acquire basic skills, and to meet the requirements for available jobs. The program contributed importantly to the increased numbers of Blacks who gained technological and professional skills in the sixties.

Whereas the disconnection between underclass Blacks and mainstream society is often clear, a somewhat more ambivalent connection exists between Black youth and the Black community. Underclass youth primarily feel a strong attachment to Black community life; it is the only arena that offers them some limited security, and it is the context in which they find cultural and ethnic resonance. The community is seen as rich in spirit, culture, and social cohesiveness but economically poor, lacking in money and power, and unable to provide needed resources. Hence, young ghetto males often both identify with and resent the community. And, as shown in Chapter Seven, their conflicting feelings are often misdirected toward the "bourgeois brothers on the hill," those Blacks who have achieved middle-classness in income and in display but who lack the real power conventionally ascribed to whites of comparable income or social status. These strivers' attempts to achieve are not the objects of the youths' criticism. Indeed, the "outfoxing"–the overcoming of mainstream barriers–is highly valued. Their disapproval applies rather to the strivers' attempts to "run the same game on the brother" as is done by the whites: using mainstream striving tactics in a Black context, with the underclass Black again the loser. They do not totally reject the striving Black, because they recognize the demands that the mainstream puts on Blacks who are achievement-bound; furthermore, even the most vociferous "antibourgeois" rhetoricians recognize that their own success, if it is to occur, will be connected in some way with the achievements of other Blacks who went before. Still, underclass males remain ambivalent about adopting what they see as the necessary "jive" posture and about meeting the unfair requirements for the abridged achievement offered to them by the mainstream.

Survival Adaptation

Finally, then, these young men demonstrate varying degrees of attachment to the dominant culture, depending on how much potential any specific short-term adaptations seems to have for helping them survive or achieve. As we have seen, many of the men adapt by keeping the ghetto as the base of functioning while holding to the dream of success within broader society. For these underclass youth, a major portion of the waking day is spent in the inner-city enclave, but almost every move related to achieving their goals is measured by mainstream standards. The men of Watts who exemplified this adaptive style were the most receptive to involvement in mainstream opportunity programs, such as antipoverty programs, since their participation was perceived as possibly leading to achievement in mainstream society.

Other men who identify more deeply with the ghetto glorify it in response to its negative valuation by the broader society. Deep empathy with the hurting brother, with the community of Blacks, leads them to refer to the common experience of exclusion as being "down" (good). They are possessive about "our way of life," even going so far as to claim title to the ghetto itself. These are the youth often identified in studies on inner-city Blacks whose primary referent is the Black context of living, those who seek there the means to survival and socioeconomic success. When looking for work, they apply to Black businesses, small shops, and local service-oriented concerns.

They also seek incomes through the deviant systems that are permitted to permeate the inner city. Much attention has focused on these illegitimate means, and much has been written about the attachment of ghetto youth to them. But the fact is that most young Blacks are not as extensively involved with these systems as has been suggested, although they know of their existence, know how to identify them, and may make periodic use of them; participation in criminal activity is primarily a means to supplement other income-gaining efforts. And much of this activity is individually acted on and poorly organized rather than carefully planned.

Thus, there are at least a few different ways to adapt to the underclass predicament. But what is significant is that these alternatives in personal style and quasi-economic striving result in no important differences in achievement. Those who seek success in the broader society in the main do not obtain it. Those who identify with Black life underachieve, because this system is underdeveloped and therefore unable to provide adequate opportunity. And those who seek security through deviant and criminal activity usually end up in jail. The problems of encapsulation for young Black males are severe, and real choices that would truly improve their future are almost nonexistent.

Nevertheless, it is not accurate to say that most have only low aspirations or that they are unmotivated, alienated, or personally deficient. They do aspire to success. They do seek achievement in the broader society. And the large majority are motivated to pursue their objectives. But the structural barriers to mainstream entry are formidable. No matter how much motivation, aspiration, or capacity they may have, the need for opportunity—and supports for achievement when there is opportunity—by far supersedes any other factor. Without a chance to make it, no amount of these personal qualities will produce large-scale achievement.

Institutional Rejection

Mainstream institutions contribute to and then reinforce the social distance from mainstream values found in ghetto youth. Detachment from mainstream ethics occurs as underclass males experience the discrepancy between what institutional rhetoric promises them and what they actually receive in terms of opportunities. Their disconnection is strengthened when they realize that it is almost impossible to influence either the programs or the practices of mainstream institutions.

Hence, ghetto youth feel convinced that these practices generate their condition of failure. Because of the covert character and impersonality of the processes of institutional rejection, it is extremely difficult, and in many cases impossible, to expose them. In view of the inability to point to the specific doers in the process, ghetto youth approach the institutions with skepticism. They do not believe they will receive fair treatment. This caution is a form of social paranoia, which on the one hand is highly functional, as it prepares the youth for rejection, a psychological readiness cushioning the pain, and on the other hand is dysfunctional, because over a long period constant readiness for rejection limits their ability to invest in programs that require a long term commitment before there is a significant pay-off. In place of serious and unguarded participation, underclass youth carry out the contact perfunctorily in anticipation of rejection, yet they seek to gain maximum reward for the period of their involvement.

Aggressive confrontation of system rejection is difficult for the individual, for the rejection processes of institutions are often devious and complex. The devices used are hidden in organizational need criteria, skill bank needs, manpower projections, and all manner of assessments of what is required for productivity. Other grounds for rejection are provided by information on the applicant's background and characteristics—his age, past work experience, educational level, and so on. Other data, such as the person's social skills, medical history, and arrest record (whether supported by subsequent prosecution and conviction or not), also serve to justify removing the seeker from job consideration.

The almost total absence of human evaluators in the rejection process intensifies the helplessness of the ghetto youth. As one young man pointed out, during the thirties and forties (which, incidentally, he thought of as ancient times), when discrimination was much more overt and not so embedded in organizational procedures, Blacks were at least able to focus their resentment accurately on those who screened them out because they were Black. It was possible to respond to discrimination and its enforcers in earlier days—whether they were overseers, straw bosses, foremen, or personnel department officers, they were identifiable actors. However, with the increasing legal prohibitions against overt racism, the exclusion began to be accomplished through institutional protocol. Now business does not deny individuals; rather, its programmed computers reject specific social profiles, and the young Black males' profiles are too commonly found in the reject track.

Employers' rejection of ghetto youth gains legitimacy when it is undergirded by references to low test scores, skill deficiencies, underdeveloped vocational plans or experience, and incomplete educations. These cited deficits add a seemingly scientific objectivity to the rejection process, allowing the institutions to transfer the burden of fault to the victims. And then the insidious game is pursued on another level, as other mainstream institutions such as universities and human services agencies develop a host of programs for intervening with rejected ghetto youth. Such programs are ostensibly aimed at remotivating the young Blacks, making up for their cultural deprivation, and reeducating them to compensate for learning disabilities; but in the end they train ghetto youth for bottom-rung jobs or for new careers in a system that still has not opened up a significant number of new career opportunities. Without being able to fully articulate all the components of what is being done, young Black males are nevertheless sensitive to them. Indeed, it is precisely the institution's denial of complicity juxtaposed with the ghetto youths' constant experience of rejection that breeds intense antagonism toward mainstream institutions.

Thus, the large-scale rejection of Black youth by white-controlled institutions of employment, education, and training has had a number of consequences. One obvious result has been the continuous growth of the underclass, whose members, even at the ages of thirteen and fourteen, are already programmed into obsolesence. This population is often referred to in documents that report on the great number of school dropouts, the numerous unemployables in the ghetto, the extensive criminality, and the increased welfare burden being assumed by the nation's cities. Black youth are identified as the problem rather than the outgrowth of their social rejection. Another result of racial rejection, particularly the insidious, impersonal kind noted previously, has been a change in the young men's attitudes toward national institutions. During the forties, period of economic expansion, lower-income young Blacks still hoped that the mainstream might let them in somewhere. But in the past couple of decades, faced with the continuing denial, many younger, poor Blacks not only have withdrawn from investing themselves in mainstream programs but have adopted a highly skeptical and, occasionally, openly hostile view of the majority's purposes. This attitude does not represent a radical change so much as a hardened opinion regarding the intention of the broader society to help eliminate the destitute condition of Blacks. It also demonstrates their strengthened belief that if one is poor and Black, one is likely to be treated unfairly by main-stream institutions.

Understanding the Rebellion

The rise in these anti-institutional feelings deeply influenced the rebellious actions of 1965, actions that revealed how racial conflicts had changed from those of the preceding decades. An examination of this period shows that antagonism between individual white citizens and Blacks (as expressed in physical confrontations) declined. In the twenties and thirties, particularly in the South, Black living areas were raided by white vigilante groups who ravaged individual males, burning, castrating, and lynching—usually finding validation in some alleged infringement of white rights by Blacks. By the forties and fifties, the nature of the conflict had changed, particularly influenced by the growth of Black urban communities, many now north of the Mason-Dixon line, and the increased presence of Black competitors in the labor force. Blacks usually responded to attacks by retaliating against individual whites, particularly those found in Black residential areas, and, in some cases, seizing goods from small local stores. These confrontations resulted in high incidences of human casualties in addition to some property loss. But as we have seen, the rebellions in the sixties, both in the objects of attack and in the actions taken, highlighted the consolidation of Blacks' reaction to the institutional and economic organization of the ghetto. Their attacks, particularly against those places that were not Black-owned (such as the burning of major supermarkets and chain stores) and which resulted in more goods being seized but fewer reprisals against individual whites, revealed a new level of social awareness.

However, this change from attacking whites to seizing goods owned by whites should not be construed to mean that in the sixties the rebellers consciously preplanned their actions or that they understood the full nature of those actions afterward. In fact, both rebels and observers often took a too-limited, and sometimes a too-extremist, position that demonstrated their confusion about the true meaning of the rebellion and the significance it would have for Black as well as for mainstream life. Some dwelled on the ferocity with which the young men burst from passive malingering and on the destructive results of this outward movement. These persons were likely to characterize the outburst as nothing but the actions of a bunch of hoodlums, alienated youth who had no investment in the community. Obviously, they misunderstood or deliberately ignored the deep roots of the rebellion and its broad impact. Others glorified the event, hailed the rebels as "street brothers" in revolution, and believed that the rebellion would bring about great changes.

This latter view was shared by some outside analysts and by most of the young rebels. Although theorists generally agree that revolts in themselves, as a form of social response, lack the ingredients for effecting profound, lasting change, some predicted that this "revolution" might manage to do so; their prediction was based on the assumption that the broader society would heed Black demands under the threat of more and larger rebellions. But they underestimated the maneuvering ability of the power structure. Similarly, the underclass youth wrongly assessed the efficacy of the revolt as a tactic for change. Their basic confusion was in believing that since their cause was just the actions they took in its support were *ipso facto* the right tactic. They held that their justified anger at racist oppression made the expression of resentment—the rebellion—a real format for reform. What they failed to understand was that the revolt only signaled the end of underclass quiescence, the refusal to tolerate any longer the systematic exclusion from the mainstream. It was not and could not become a substitute for programs aimed at basic alterations in the ghetto, particularly in the relationship between the ghetto and the broader society.

The explosion only temporarily interrupted the daily exploitation, it did not prepare the rebels for governing the ghetto. Their actions stimulated mainstream institutional withdrawal, created a void in the control and service delivery patterns of many ghetto organizations, and clearly broke the traditional ties with municipal and county officialdom. But they lacked both the tools and the power to move forward after the break. They were not prepared to respond adequately to the departure of private business. Neither were they able to compete with the recalcitrant city government, which refused to initiate reparative programs or even to force the responsible agencies to make available or reinstitute municipal services such as public utilities, sanitation, rubble removal, traffic and street lights, and public transportation. The combination of private business withdrawal and public agency irresponsiveness guaranteed that the already underserviced ghetto residents would receive only minimal services, if any at all. And the void created by mainstream institutional withdrawal was never adequately refilled. Despite a programmatic articulation of self-help, the rebels were unable to effectively replace or to encourage large-scale replacement of abandoned businesses and services.

The failure of early post-rebellion restoration activity was due mainly to the absence of preplanning. The immediate problems—developing an ideological position regarding ghetto restoration and creating the necessary strategies for carrying it out—required answers to several important questions: Should Blacks seek to control the economic and social organizations of the inner-city ghetto? If so, how should they proceed? If they succeeded, could they then use this controlled sphere as a power base from which to negotiate changes in broader society's institutions? How much political energy should be concentrated on rebuilding the inner city and how much on filling mainstream openings resulting from the revolt? Who from the Black community should fill those positions? The essential issue was which paths to follow in the quest for Black mobility. Unfortunately, however, because of the internal differences among Blacks described previously, and because the rebels lacked ideological clarity, political skills, and effective power, the answers to these questions were largely taken from their hands. Broader society reasserted its control, first of all, by responding to the rebellion with a quick and massive display of "law and order"; later, alert to the Black community's inner turmoil, they supported those who deemphasized Black community governance. Mainstream eventually covered up the hole it had left in the ghetto with a number of palliative rehabilitation and training programs, which were offered to the underclass youth as a "potential" way out of ghetto confinement.

Two elements crucial to effective implementation of this combined mainstream approach were the readiness of the inner-city poor to accept almost any programs offered to relieve their severe condition of need and the recruitment of many Blacks to administer and in other ways uncritically "honcho" these programs with the underclass. Through such programs, broader society demonstrated its alertness to underclass explosiveness and conveyed its concern with the social basis of ghetto uprisings; and, by enlisting middle-class and striving Blacks (many of whom later obtained mainstream positions), it reaffirmed to its members, particularly middle America, a continued commitment to a national policy of containing Blacks in the central cities while providing them only limited access to the mainstream. In the end, these antipoverty programs, the only hope the poor had left for escape from ghetto encapsulation, failed to produce any significant underclass mobility or, even further, to alter the disfavored position of inner-city institutions vis-a-vis mainstream institutions.

Impact of the Revolts—the New Blackness

Irrespective of the influence that ideological inexperience had in shaping the strategies adopted by the rebels, it is politically short-sighted not to critically examine the widespread effects (including new perspectives) of the rebellions on Black life, and on the national scene as well.

Social analysts have largely been silent concerning the positive impact of the rebellions on American politics. In part, their practice of omitting positive references to these activities is due to the belief that reporting constructive results would only encourage further uprisings. Others have suggested that the silence is due to the improbability of mainstream analysts' finding positives in an action aimed at destroying mainstream's advantage over the inner-city poor. After all, this advantaged relationship is one that establishment observers are inclined by their own socialization to support.

Notwithstanding the general failure of both Blacks and whites to acknowledge their impact, analysis of the 1965 rebellions shows that they did affect not only the traditional relationship between mainstream and the ethnic poor but, more particularly, the perspectives among Blacks themselves. Once a rebellion occurred in a ghetto, Black community life was never again the same. One important factor was that the explosions primarily involved younger "have not" underclass males. The age and social class of the rebels, the form of protest, and the objects of destruction all served to force new considerations in the politics and social organization of Black life. Another important factor was the inability of the Black community to offer any significant substitute for the Civil Rights movement, which, in effect, was killed along with its leader by 1968. The death of this protest movement meant there was no longer any civil rights vehicle to counter antiliberal forces and to meet the needs of impoverished youth in the twentieth century.

The explosive emergence of the community's poor highlighted the differences in social values among the more stable working element, the middle-income Blacks (particularly those who functioned primarily in mainstream life), and the encapsulated "street brothers." These differences formed the base of the substantive political issues to be resolved during the next five to six years. From 1965 through 1970, one of the most dramatic public occurrences in Black life took place: the forging of a new social contract articulating the relationship of Blacks with white society and Blacks with Blacks. An entirely new posture as an ethnic, political, special-interest group was established.

Parts of the changes that Blacks underwent were stimulated by the emergency quality of underclass demands for a new attitude toward protest and, indeed, for the creation of a new Black man. They were committed to never again accept violent personal attacks from those who resisted the equality of Blacks in society. Turning the other cheek and passive resistance were not acceptable as a posture for Black struggles. In its place Blacks demanded that new rules be created to govern Black participation in American life. And they called on Blacks as a group to find new ways to relate to one another and to determine their own goals and activities. In many ways the desperation and broad scope of the demands were generated by the knowledge that if the old format of race relations were continued Blacks would still be closed out of the opportunity system of society and would be made to remain quiescent within the ghetto.

In a somewhat unusual way, the ideological issues arising from this quest for a new Black man involved not only a political reposturing but a psychological metamorphosis. For to move from Negro to Black politics required a movement from a Negro to a Black perspective. White America likes to think of the difficulty it had in coming to grips with the new Black man of the sixties; however, it seldom considered the powerful experience this change represented for Blacks themselves. Many new concepts to underpin Blackness and self-determination emerged. Negritude and connections with Africa—other than the American past of slavery and its consequential second-class status—were examined. Out of these came new perceptions of Blacks' connections with American society, a new concept of negritude in America known as blackness, a new vocabulary, and a new way of thinking. The articulations of Blacks were expressed in new metaphor; they projected new images from a positive indigenous viewpoint, as exemplified in the love song by Roberta Flack in which she urges her lover to "be real Black for me."

As a new group identity grew more solid, the means of manifesting the group's demands became a subject of much debate. Out of this came a concern with the role of Black institutions in the thrust for equality, a reassessment of the propriety of using mainstream organizations to express Black views, and a reexamination of the feasibility of developing viable Black programs through "integrated" organizations. The principle that legitimate Black interests could not be represented by other than Blacks, the legitimacy and efficacy of Blacks meeting alone as Blacks to plan strategies, the right of Blacks as a special-interest group to consider the issues affecting their destiny, and the principle that programs to influence the status of Blacks could not legitimately be implemented without Blacks' participation— these became the new ethics guiding Black-white relations and represented one thrust in a newly emerging ethnic politics.

These principles and rights were put into operation by means of Black political caucuses. In "integrated" organizations, the caucus structure allowed separate planning and ethnic-group advocacy. Later this format became standard not only among Blacks but among almost all other minority groups in search of their rights. Through this development, Blacks and others achieved some political clout, forcing institutions to somewhat modify their traditional procedures to make allowances for ethnic and minority concerns. In almost all areas of mainstream life, in government, in education, in private firms, the interests of Blacks, particularly in eliminating institutional racist practices, were articulated and fought for through caucus organizations. Some other changes initiated in the sixties continue to influence contemporary political relationships, not only between Blacks and broader society but between almost all deprived groups and the mainstream. And some social movements of the seventies, such as the women's rights movement, have found inspiration in and have borrowed from Black political strategies of the mid-sixties.

Out of the rebellions came some other important changes, too, such as a new concern with community development. Heretofore, breaking down the barriers to mainstream entry had been the chief goal of Black activity, but now recognition of the serious problem created by the general decay of the inner city, accompanied by the swiftly growing underclass, forced Blacks to pay more attention to the economic state of ghetto life itself. The economic destitution of the inner city became a cornerstone of the community's reparative activity. The condition of a large class of obsolete young male adults trapped and unattended in the heart of the city represented a threat to the community's stability, as well as to its survival.

Another group profoundly influenced was the Black social science community. Encouraged by new currents within Black life and by the underclass redefinition of both Black-Black and Black-white cultural and political relations, Black professionals began to examine many traditional notions concerning Black life-styles, community organizing principles, interpersonal and family relationships, and Black psychology and beliefs. For example, new importance was given to ethnicity as a factor in Black oppression and to liberation strategies as against class factors; positive ethnocentrism was elevated in contrast with the former emphasized deviant-subculture thesis. Most important was the reaffirmation of the Black family structure, and one's function therein, as a prime contributor to Blacks' survival. This emphasis replaced the persistent notion promulgated by mainstream social scientists that the Negro family was in disarray and that in fact it was the primary source of the second-class position of Blacks and the conveyor of a disadvantaged culture.

New approaches to social science research, particularly involving minority populations, were initiated by Black social scientists. And ultimately many new issues emerged from their studies, while new concepts and outlooks developed to undergird this research. From 1966 to 1975, Black social science literature proliferated at an unprecendated rate. Particularly significant, the literature represented a profound examination of the Black experience, much of it from a Black perspective.

More important than the explosion itself, however, was the posture adopted afterward by the rebels. In contrast with some forecasts, the majority did not immediately return to their earlier behaviors and games. Paradoxically, in spite of their rebellion, the participants were urged to become active community helping agents. Encouraged by the belief that they had performed a noble deed, motivated by an opportunity to participate, and stimulated by Black leaders' seeming failure to respond to the inner-city disarray left by the rebellion, these men sought to influence the directions and programs of community redevelopment. In Watts, for example, the rebels formed the Sons of Watts, which represented a real departure from their traditional deviant adaptation and signified the entry of underclass men into the social and political life of the community. Despite efforts by the media to discredit the Sons as a positive social force in

Watts—primarily because it maintained elements of gang structure, because it did not function as a conventional organization, and because some of its members retained connections with systems of illegitimate income—the organization did play a significant part in developing programs after the rebellion. As an indigenous group, the Sons of Watts provided opportunities for underclass men to express themselves, and it became a catalyst in awakening the sociopolitical awareness of the community. At the height of its existence (1965–1970), the Sons probably had one of the most dramatic impacts on Watts of any local organization and represented for many jobless, poor, and low-income young men a vehicle through which to transmit their views.

Conclusion

Finally, then, the rebellions and the actions that resulted from them did have an impact on Blacks' political attitudes toward mainstream life and organizations. Equally significant was the public reassertion of the real economic condition of Blacks throughout the nation. Despite the continuous protests of Blacks since the forties about their entrapment in ghettos and about not being allowed equal economic opportunity, mainstream continued to propagate the belief that Blacks, like all other Americans, were swiftly moving into the middle class. This myth of wide-ranging Black mobility was cited as evidence that America was truly becoming a fully integrated, equal-opportunity society. But the rebellions that spread across the nation from 1965 to 1968 exposed to all the extent of deprivation and confinement that a large section of Blacks were no longer able to endure. The central city ghetto did not house only a small number of newly arrived poor rural Blacks in migratory transition; rather it had become the enclave in which a disproportionately large number of the nation's Blacks were enclosed, experiencing a continuous resource drain and receiving very little attention.

Despite some positive consequences of the rebellions, little significant improvement has occurred in the condition of the poor since 1965. Current examination of inner-city life shows that the problems of a decade ago remain the problems of today, only now they are more impacted. The basic poverty reflected in long-term underemployment and unemployment, low and minimum incomes, and social destitution continues to persist. The idle and unused in the community are increasingly visible, but there is no corresponding decrease in the weight of high rent, food, and insurance prices. The community's institutions—its social service agencies and its legal, educational, and employment programs—also bend under the weight of high demand and insufficient resources. In short, the community struggles with an inordinate amount of social stress and severely limited options.

Continuing to play a major role in the increased problems of the inner city is mainstream's policy of "benign neglect." Crime control agents are a major resource for diffusing ghetto unrest with their constant contact with and surveillance of underclass activity. However, when teamed with the rest of the legal machinery—the courts and the bail and probation systems— they are able to confine Black youth not only within the ghettos but also within jails and prisons (where today it is well known that the proportion of Blacks to whites is much higher than in the general population). Ultimately, such practices seek to render these young men quiescent and invisible. And supplementing this paramilitary "law and order" is a network of equally contradictory agencies and rehabilitation programs, including those labeled narcotics control and alcoholism treatment. Broader society expends major resources to control the underclass through these programs, but the underclass continues to grow through inattention to increasing joblessness, federal dissociation from aggressive affirmative action programs, and the limited availability of funds that support energetic inner-city redevelopment. Mainstream neglect produces a resource void in the inner cities, which in turn reinforces "retributive justice" and establishes a stress cycle exemplified by that associated with the explosions of the sixties.

More recently, a new pressure has afflicted the poor of the inner cities. For over a decade after the explosions, the ghettos were allowed to lie dormant in decay; now, however the city has become a prime area for relocating whites. The influx of younger generation whites in search of metropolitan conveniences has heralded the return of small businesses, the flow of monies from banks to areas previously redlined (systematically denied bank loans), the rise in the cost and value of housing, and the increased reclamation of dwellings by absentee owners for private use or for resale. The housing problems of the poor have become critical as more and more are being pushed out of their traditional multidwelling inner-city rental units without either practical means for relocating or housing programs that meet their needs.

The magnitude of the problem that this stagnating group represents to both mainstream society and the community of Blacks is being increasingly exposed. Despite the surface effectiveness of the ghetto-fence policy, breakdowns, particularly from overloads in ancillary maintenance systems, continue to come to public awareness. People are becoming more and more alarmed about the deep-seated unrest that permeates the underclass, about the outbreaks of social protest in the prison system where they are housed, and about the mass looting that occurs whenever the reins of external control are rendered ineffective, such as during natural disasters or city blackouts.

It is clear that those who have been systematically denied mainstream opportunity will not be able, under normal circumstances, to significantly alter their conditions. The existence of a national economy that refuses to seek full employment and that resists an expanded work force supports charges that underclass people are society's unusables, surplus labor in a market already filled to capacity.

To overcome the conditions faced by the underclass, the nation must make significant efforts to revitalize the inner cities and to redirect programs toward providing income for the able-bodied poor and subsequently offering increased opportunity for mobility. Without earning power and without a fair chance for betterment, the Black poor can never be said to have participated in the American dream and the Black community will be continually laden with the burden of national racism.

10

||||||||||||||||||||||||||||||||||||||||||||||||||||||||||||||||||||||||||||||||||||||||||||||

Reversing Underclass Growth

||||||||||||||||||||||||||||||||||||||||||||||||||||||||||||||||||||||||||||||||||||||||||||||

It is clear, then, that in the eighties the primary aim both of Black action and of national efforts to deal with the underclass crisis must be to provide jobs, both inside as well as outside the inner city. First and foremost, young Blacks need employment that provides not only the important experience of work but also a livable income. Programs that do not significantly increase their incomes cannot alter the condition of the poor and, by extension, the condition of the ghetto. Job programs that are not connected to the primary job market provide no avenues for advancement and movement up in the job world and, at best, can provide only temporary relief. No amount of social rehabilitation, community participation, or motivational programs will substitute for being able to earn a way with self-respect.

A Record of National Response

Creating real work opportunities and providing livable incomes were the principal ingredients missing in the antipoverty programs from 1961 through 1975. During this period, administrations representing the full political spectrum articulated

173

programs that were ostensibly a response to the plight of the inner-city poor. The death of John Kennedy prevented full development of his administration's approach to ghetto revitalization. However, in the name of mental health, various proposals were offered to eradicate what was then identified as a social cancer fed by a poverty culture. The elimination of this cultural legacy and its components was to be pivotal in the destruction of poverty. Thus the rehabilitative, motivational, and compensatory programs initiated in the early sixties that aimed to improve ghetto residents' capacity to compete in the mainstream's labor market, although laudable, did not offer jobs in the end and left hundreds of thousands of youthful Blacks economically dependent.

The state of poor Blacks continued to worsen. Finally during Lyndon Johnson's tenure, the inner cities exploded in protest against continued joblessness, ghetto confinement, and the anticipated demise of the civil rights movement. The hoax of rehabilitation without the reality of opportunity, the years of evasive social reform, and the ultimate anger at not being able to enter the broader society, especially after having one's hopes raised, provided one of the crucial elements for rebellion. In response, the Johnson administration promised to wage a full-scale war against poverty. The Office of Economic Opportunity (OEO) was created "to eliminate poverty" by (1) retraining the poor to assume more responsibility for their lives and communities—to be done through a greater citizen participation in the organization and affairs of the community—and (2) improving opportunity for those from poor areas who had skills—to be accomplished through an "affirmative action" policy aimed at breaking the patterns of institutional resistance that served to exclude Blacks and other ethnic minorities from equal access and opportunity.

The War on Poverty has been subjected to voluminous analysis. Basically, the findings show that the war was lost; as a measure to create new opportunities for poor ghetto dwellers, it was a failure. When training was undertaken, it was generally limited to lower-level or dead-end jobs. And even when ghetto youth entered these training programs and were considered to have completed them successfully, they did not find significant employment. In the end, then, the War on Poverty made no substantial inroads into the growth of the underclass; neither did it appreciably reverse the direction of youthful Blacks' underemployment and unemployment. One important factor influencing this was that despite encouragement by the federal government private industry was little involved in the training, and, later, hiring of the trainees.

The ghetto uprisings, as we have seen, had a pronounced effect on American sentiments. "Backlash" politics, which was the open expression of white America's view that Blacks and other minorities were receiving too much attention from national and state governments, became the order of the day. The Democrats were voted out of office, accused, among other things, of being too lenient with Blacks. The Republicans, with Richard Nixon at the helm, were given support for using a firmer hand, and they responded with a sweeping effort to bring quiet to the inner cities. Ghetto unrest was answered with "law and order." The offices that included the programs for the War on Poverty were systematically dismantled. Direct federal funds for reconstruction and indigenous-group programs were withdrawn. Ultimately, these and other social rehabilitation funds were redistributed in lump-sum amounts to the state governments under a revenue-sharing plan that effectively removed control of this money from inner-city and antipoverty groups. These funds then became part of the pooled monies that could be sought by all organizations, including state agencies. A limited amount of money was earmarked especially for use by the poor. In fact, over time, much of the money from revenue sharing was funneled into programs to support the law and order policy in the cities.

The primary plank in the administration's platform covering the poor was welfare reorganization. The essentials of this policy were harbored in two proposed program changes: the Family Assistance Program (FAP), which was to replace the older, Aid to Families with Dependent Children (AFDC) program, and Workfare, which was aimed at revising the work-related component of welfare. Under FAP, restrictions were placed on the outside income allowances of welfare recipients, and eligibility was tied to work. Such changes were basically punitive rather than ameliorative, destroying incentives to work, since most often if work was found it would be in the second-ary, low-wage labor market. In addition, any limited income from work would result in a commensurate decrease in welfare payments, thereby rendering the recipient family no better off than in its prework condition. This program did nothing to re-duce the condition of poverty and underclassness. The admini-stration did provide some support to the Black community through the "Black capitalism" program, under which individ-ual Black entrepreneurs could get small-business loans to either expand existing enterprises or develop new ones. Though this program was utilized by some Blacks to start up new businesses, it did not really make a dent in the huge problem of economic underdevelopment in the ghetto. Most of all, very few jobs for young Blacks resulted from it. The Ford administration that followed Nixon's demise offered no programmatic innovation or change in approaching the urban crisis. Hence, neither politi-cal party provided the leadership or programmatic approach to eradicate the underclass. Compensatory interventions alone were not effective; neither were social participation and skills train-ing, workfare, reorganized welfare, nor pump-priming Black capitalism effective means to counter underclass growth. By emphasizing quiet in the ghettos, Nixon's law and order prac-tices allowed the nation's majority to hope that the inner-city problem had abated, but, in fact, it had increased. All these ap-proaches missed the basic target: creating programs that would assure young Blacks entry into the primary labor market.

The Carter Administration Proposals

It remains to be seen whether Jimmy Carter's administra-tion can do better, although all indications are that it will not. Examination of the proposed urban plan discloses two major strategies—again, welfare reform, including the provision of work, and a comprehensive urban renewal program. Since both programs are intended to be phased in over several years, their true impact would not be felt until the early eighties (1983 is the forecast). The attendant publicity seeks to assure the public that these efforts will not cost more than present means to support the poor and may even cost less over a period of time.

There could be a promising note in these proposals, as the combination of changing the welfare system and, as a part of that, developing employment opportunities does have potential for reversing the growth of the underclass. And there is no doubt that something must be done about welfare; the existing system is liked by neither administrators nor taxpayers, and its inequities move even the clients to rebel against it. Yet welfare reform, as represented in the first reactions by Congress and other interested national bodies to H.R.9030, will not be a major alteration but rather will continue the practice of making incremental changes. In addition, the primary resource needed to undergird the work provisions—private industry—has once again demonstrated great resistance to serious involvement. Consequently, the only area that holds potential to create jobs is the federal sector—and this in the public services area. As is well known, public-sponsored job programs, as exemplified by the OEO under Nixon, are only as lasting as is the administration. A change in the national political climate or in administration can easily result in these programs being terminated. But, in any case, welfare reform can never substitute for economic opportunity. Jobs, access to the primary labor market, and earned income are the real bases for a lasting cure.

Relation of Ghetto Youth to Welfare System

Unfortunately, the term "welfare reform" has become in the minds of many Americans a euphemism for the politics of the poor, the Black poor in particular. And reform over the past two decades, coincident with the worsening condition of the urban poor, has meant taking punitive measures against the needy. Thus in addressing the issue of welfare reform, three myths perpetuated by the mainstream persist about the characteristics of underclass youth and about their involvement in the welfare structure. Two of these myths were discussed earlier, but they deserve reiteration here.

Myth 1: Poor Black Males Lack Goals and Motivation to Succeed. In brief, the Watts study shows that ghetto youth are motivated to achieve on various levels in the work world, although they tend to be unclear about the many vocational fields available and about how to attain their aims. More significant, the findings reveal that the absence of significant role models in their daily lives affects not only what they aspire to but what they achieve. The separation between Black achievers and underclass males often influences the youths' aspirations, as the absence of ties with effective "honchos" (that is, with persons within the mainstream job world) often determines their selection of alternative paths for achievement. In the end, the single most important deterent to achievement was found to be the process of institutional rejection combined with the system's collusion in reinforcing the condition of nonmobility.

Myth 2: They Do Not Want Work. No more devious belief about a group has been popularized than the one which asserts that the youthful Black poor do not want to work. What in fact has occurred is that the system has blamed the victims for its own faults. Clearly, factors endemic to the nation's economy—cybernated production, automation, greater reliance on technology, and an unexpanding domestic market, particularly in labor-intensive work areas—create and maintain the underclass. The lack of opportunity for work and the concomitant search for any means to economically survive are two factors that eventually frame the attitudes of the rejected. The idealism of work is stunted by the reality of no work. Yet young Blacks are said to prefer welfare to work. Some are less than enthusiastic about work, while others have come to totally despise work and assuredly do not seek it, since it means tedium of subsistence pay and nonproductive jobs. The Watts study found that, primarily, the experience of institutional rejection frustrates, angers, and steals away the desire to pursue work enthusiastically and, at the same time, encourages the search for alternative ways to secure a living.

Myth 3: Underclass Youth Constitute a Major Part of the Welfare Population. Throughout this book, little has been said about the attachment of underclass youth to the system of welfare. This may appear strange, when it is known that governmental income-maintenance programs are a main source of money for the ghetto poor. It seems ever more strange when one realizes that almost all the media in the nation identify poor Blacks as the principal welfare problem and thus a tax burden. The reason for the lack of discussion is simple: although most people are not aware of this fact, Black males ages fifteen to twenty-four are most often *not* eligible for welfare programs, particularly those supposedly aimed at assisting the poor. Like other mainstream institutions, the system of welfare rejects them and exacerbates their condition of helplessness. Not only does it deny eligibility to underclass young men, it forces them to cut natural family ties and ultimately reinforces their dependency and socially dysfunctional adaptations.

Analysis of federal support programs for the poor from 1965 through 1975 shows that the single largest program was Aid to Families with Dependent Children (AFDC), which over the years has come to resemble a patchwork of revisions, sometimes affecting eligibility, payment scales, or changes in supplements. Currently AFDC covers young persons eighteen years and over only if they are regularly attending school or taking a vocational or technical course. For young men under eighteen who are not living with their parents and are not under some governmental agency guardianship, no form of federal public assistance exists. Underclass males (particularly those typical of this study populations) who neither reside in their parents' homes nor go to school are ineligible for this federally sponsored program.

Likewise, these youth do not get much benefit from most social services programs, which presently are organized under Title XX of the Social Security Act and the Comprehensive Employment and Training Act (CETA). From a federal perspective, one need only meet certain income criteria and very broad need standards in order to be eligible. But the legislation allows states (in the case of Title XX) and prime sponsors (CETA) to define

their own services and target groups within broad federal guidelines, according to their own local standards and program assessments. Therefore, since young unmarried Blacks even in the
CETA program are rarely considered to have high employment
potential, they are generally relegated to the lowest rung in the
priority ladder. Although underclass youth may be included in
one of the four categories having federal priority (veterans, the
economically disabled, the unemployed, the underemployed),
they are rarely considered for either the public service jobs or
the on-the-job-training slots. Few states offer social services for
able-bodies youths unless they are part of AFDC households or
part of the juvenile or child welfare systems. Preventive social
services are almost unknown for this group.

And what about certain other programs that do not fall
under public assistance but nevertheless might provide some
help to underclass youth under welfare insurance programs,
such as the survivors' insurance plan of Old Age Survivors Disability Insurance (OASDI), the pension program for dependents
of deceased veterans, and unemployment compensation? The
first two support any insured family whose income was interrupted by the death of a breadwinner, but they are intended to
help children in a dependent state, not emancipated young men.
These men are of course eligible for unemployment compensation if they have worked for the required period and not been
fired, but many do not meet these criteria, since they have been
unable to find long-term employment.

The only welfare sources from which underclass youth
stand to gain are the surplus commodities and the food stamp
programs of the Department of Agriculture. Since one can qual-
ify for these if his income is low enough, the single person is
eligible for food stamps without regard to age. Presently, however, food stamps must be purchased with cash on a regular
basis, and thus again the young ghetto dweller may be excluded
because he has so little cash. Congress has passed a bill that
would eliminate the purchase requirement, but enactment of
the bill alone, without other broad-ranging efforts to cure the
condition of the underclass, will simply do nothing more than
prevent this population from starving.

In view of these facts, how can it be alleged that those who are the least-direct users of welfare programs, who are in fact ineligible in most cases, place a heavy drain on the public through welfare attachment? Surely this myth is perpetuated to hide the fact that it is the exclusion of this group from real work opportunity, and at the same time most social welfare benefits, that creates their severe economic impotence and social dysfunction. Any time a society keeps such a large body of young able-bodied males out of the opportunity system, it not only causes deprivation but renders them less able to perform the socially expected functions, that is, to hold down jobs, to secure credit, and to plan families and adequately provide for them.

Yet, the underclass does exact a high cost from society for its maintenance, and this cost is found in wasted manpower, nonproductive citizens, and in the expenditures of the nation's social institutions such as the courts and prisons, which each day devote more and more time to process and maintain this population. And with even greater intensity, the larger community of Blacks and its organizational apparatus absorb the weight and cost of this population. And too, although the underclass male has few formal attachments to welfare, he is indirectly dependent, as was discussed in Chapter Six. He obtains money by forming relationships of various kinds with women who are eligible for public assistance. But because of long-standing welfare policies, which declare that a woman will not receive aid if there is an employable man in the house, these relationships often become tenuous at best. The young man may continually leave the family he is a part of, or more typically, come home only when it is thought that social investigators will not be checking households for evidence of "a man in the house." This common practice affords the family continuous eligibility, but it also effectively erodes the stability and integrity of the underclass family. Moreover, the dependence of the young Black male on the female, in a society that honors the providers and awards status and credit eligibility to the income earner, cannot help but create significant problems in these relationships. Although more recently the "man in the house" provision has been removed in thirty-six states and although this action represents a step in the right direction, it still does little to address the basic problem of the Black male. Thus, although he may now remain with the family without jeopardizing its welfare support, he continues to be a burden—unemployed and economically impotent. In this way, the difficulties produced by broader society and exacerbated by welfare policies ultimately affect the Black family structure and its interactional patterns more than does any hypothesized "poverty culture."

Despite the need for welfare assistance programs to be reformed—that is, updated and brought into conjunction with present day socio-economic realities—the community of Blacks should not allow the politics of welfare to govern their actions, since welfare reform will not really provide the economics and job base needed to reverse underclass growth. Although liberal and professional groups and even recipient movements have argued for the "right to welfare," as noted earlier, the fact is that whether it is or not a right, far too many Black families have become inextricably trapped in this system as their only means of survival. Welfare has become a principal method by which society is able to maintain large numbers of Black at subsistence levels of income. By being attached to this system, many have never had complete control of their lives. In the absence of any realistic alternative, they remain at the mercy of those who manipulate these programs, who ostensibly are responding to the needs of the poor but whose real concern is with regulating, controlling, and maintaining the poor. Continually there are increases in assistance payments, then reductions; provision of food stamps free, then making them available at a cost; making social services mandatory, sometimes voluntary, but more often not available; realignment of payment scales based on government indexes, then readjusting them in response to political pressures. In this endless seesawing, the poor are manipulated and thousands of Black families in ghettos across the nation are negatively affected.

Most often the social work profession, welfare rights organizations, and other client-advocate groups have concentrated on modifying practices or removing certain inadequacies or inequities in existing programs. For example, these groups have

exerted considerable effort over the past decade to boost payment scales, establish new eligibility categories, and increase
ancillary benefits, such as food stamps and medical coverage.
These efforts are laudable, yet they should be recognized for
what they truly are. They make modifications in the existing
network, and, to the degree that these changes minimize the
pain that users experience or increase the benefits or services
available in any given program, they are positive efforts and
should be supported. However, rearrangement of existing programs will not address the all-important issues of jobs and stable
incomes and hence the problem of eradicating underclass
growth.

Ultimately, a different method altogether of addressing
the income needs of the poor is required. Various proposals
have been considered to a limited degree. One suggests an annual tax credit, perhaps to be administered by the Internal
Revenue Service. Much earlier, similar schemes, such as the
guaranteed annual income and the regressive tax plans were
discussed. A major stumbling block to their adoption has been
to find agreement on the definition of what constitutes an adequate income and which populations would be eligible. Notwithstanding the need for clearer definition, this direction of response for income to the poor who are not available for work
holds much promise; it would recognize the financial needs of
the poor, separate income considerations from service needs and
employ a system that would potentially be more responsive to
the dynamics of inflation and recession.

Lest we forget, dependence on welfare as the means to
correct the ills of the youthful underclass is a mistake not only
for the mainstream but also for poor Blacks as well. There is an
increasing tendency for certain members of deprived groups to
feel that society owes them something since it has systematically deprived them of their natural rights as citizens. Although
this argument is often useful in obtaining overdue benefits, it
fosters the belief that public assistance is a right, and therefore
reliance on this system to meet the poor community's needs is
an understandable reaction. But having a "welfare psychology"
("somebody owes me something") also leads to the delusion
that society will, if reminded enough, eventually provide a pub-

lic assistance program capable of adequately supporting an individual and his or her family. Nothing is less likely. Public assistance must never be accepted as the primary source of income by Black work-capable citizens.

The Weight Is on the Black Community

As the decade of the seventies ends, the task of securing equal opportunity and economic equity for young Blacks is no less difficult now than in the past. Certainly, racism, no matter how deeply hidden in institutional practices or how covertly manifested, in combination with the nation's pattern of limited domestic market expansion, remains the chief cause of the underclass status of such vast numbers of young Black males. The community of Blacks in the eighties faces the enormous job of seizing the initiative to reverse underclass growth. To do this, at minimum, action must be directed at achieving three major goals. The first must be to create and support legislative actions aimed at breaking the unemployment crisis of Black youth. The second involves use of legislative and political power to create government action to free up resources for use in a comprehensive urban restoration program. And third, there must be greater efforts by Blacks themselves to develop a broad network of inner-city agencies—economic, social, and cultural—capable of providing a greater portion of the needed services to these communities.

Jobs for the Underclass

Once again we return to the basic issue: If this nation is to break underclassness and its accompanying social ills it must provide opportunities for young Blacks to become attached to a sound system of income and mobility. Just as private industry employment provides this basic security for most people, so it must for poor Blacks too. Achieving this goal is no easy accomplishment. An examination of those employers who could be instrumental in making a massive national job program successful reveals a very disheartening picture. The private sector has refused in the past to become fully committed to training programs and even less to jobs for the poor. Large corporations remain aloof to the critical need to expand employment and to make special efforts to provide work for inner-city youth. The business community continues to be more concerned with keeping the labor force as small as possible, while extracting maximum gain from the system of production.

The labor movement has also shown little support for increased employment, particularly for programs through which the poor might become union members and thereby obtain the benefits secured by most workers. The absence of any significant labor role in the training programs of the sixties and the present hesitancy to address the issue of unemployment unless it affects union members do not suggest that labor plans any important involvement in programs of work for underemployed ghetto youth.

Congress too, despite its continued expressions of concern about the level of national unemployment, has been noticeably slow in attacking this problem wholesale. Some initiatives have been taken, as in the much-weakened Humphrey-Hawkins bill, H.R.50, which passed Congress by having gained support from both the private sector and labor for a full-employment policy. But the provisions of this bill are meaningless if not made functional in a way that addresses the problems special to the Black underclass. For example, when legislation such as H.R. 50 provides for "an acceptable national level of unemployment" of 4 percent, this should apply to Blacks in proportion to their numbers in society. At best, if there is to be equity, even in unemployment, then Black youth would shoulder their "acceptable" level of unemployment (4 percent) and not be, as is now the case, disproportionately burdened with anywhere from 40 to 65 percent unemployment. Such a proportional change in Black unemployment would be a clear indication of the underclass being dissolved and would enhance immeasurably the ability of the Blacks to more readily and less painfully help meet their community's needs.

Unfortunately, the current administration has not been in the forefront of activities to deal with unemployment, placing its energies in trying to halt inflation instead. But in the end, the government will have to provide the initiative in the jobs program and even provide many of the jobs for the poor, at least to begin with. It may not be everybody's favorite idea, but it represents the reality of current economic politics, since neither business nor labor seems committed to opening up jobs for the excluded underclass. Federal initiative could result in an effective start-up program if clear guidelines are established early. Such a program should seek to achieve: (1) acceptance of the government as the initiator but not as the long-term carrier of the poor; (2) jobs that are not the usual dead-end types with only marginal incomes; they should pay a living wage, offer on-the-job-training, and, when experience and skill are gained, provide opportunity for transfers to jobs in the primary labor market that ensure seniority, and union protection; and (3) affirmative action to break the disproportionate unemployment common among Black youth. Without this, the burden of unemployment will continue, inequitably, to be shouldered by Black youth.

The reasons for these goals are obvious. The crisis of young Blacks precipitated by mass unemployment can only be adequately responded to by quick emergency federal actions to create jobs, most likely in the public services area. Yet it is wholly useless to attempt to create incentives to work if such work is only temporary or simply a perpetuation of low-income experience. Thus those jobs that are created should be recognized as fulfilling the need for employment and providing income, but they must also be seen as start-up jobs that lead to employment in the primary labor market of both the public and private sectors.

Whatever combination of programs is used to break the entrapped condition of the underclass, there must also be a national commitment to undertake the task and to accept the necessary costs and energies; otherwise, the poor will remain a social burden. There is no inexpensive way to undo what institutionalized racism and a nation's economic organization has done to a significant portion of the nation's citizens. And unless both labor and industry are given incentives to join in this endeavor, support of the poor will continue to fall to individual taxpayers. Incentives should be provided to business not only for job development but also for training and ultimately for creating new domestic job markets. Failure to develop jobs that furnish adequate income for the able-bodied poor will further nurture the social conflict between the haves and have nots, the income earners and the impoverished, the rich and the poor; and when racism is a major determinant of who has and who has not, that conflict will be between Black and white.

Urban Development

The second major push is to mount legislative actions for a *comprehensive* program for urban development and inner-city restoration. This program is essential, for without city-based comprehensive planning, without federal dollars to support inner-city and urban area development, and without these dollars (resources) being channeled to inner-city agencies, the banks and large business interests will remain in control of urban growth patterns. As earlier noted, the current administration's Urban Development program, projected to impact by the eighties and not to be costly, has in most ways failed to emerge. Noticeably, no one comprehensive plan was submitted to Congress for action. Instead, the administration sought for piecemeal passage of some urban-related bills and for reallocation of prior committed program monies, using a policy of fiscal restraint. Despite some limited, yet notable, success, such as in the passage of the Urban Development Actions Grants (UDAG), which provides funds for private and public joint action in community development, the administration's approach to urban development did not receive favorable attention from Congress. The failure to provide a comprehensive rubric for urban development, the lack of city planning framed within such guidelines, and the absence of inner-city interests in the planning process and in related programs has resulted in the flow of urban funds to cities becoming highly politicized. It also precludes effective, coordinated use of federal resources, as piecemeal programming ultimately serves only to proliferate independent—noncoordinated—bureaucratic activity. Under such conditions, the inner-city poor are the ones who remain powerless, unable to affect their living environment. Ultimately they get squeezed out.

Inner-City Education

In the past two decades, the inner-city school system has had a devastating impact on Black youths; it has failed to educate, train, socialize, or in other ways to help them become successful achievers. That one out of every three inner-city child faces educational failure is catastrophic and reflects a deep-seated national problem. The research cited in Chapter Four provides some insight into factors contributing to the deplorable statistics. For example, the inner-city school propagates mainstream success and values while it conveys to Black youths that their own social context is worthless; it attempts to socialize the youngster to anticipate mainstream achievement yet is unable to provide clear paths to this attainment. Ghetto-entrapped youths defend their personal and ethnic integrity by confrontation and disassociation. The consequence is ultimately failure. And even for those who do adopt mainstream goals, no guarantee of success exists, for limited opportunities, restricted market need, racism, and the lack of connection of ghetto schools (as a feeder organization) to the job market continue to further the underattainment of Black youths.

This book does not seek to offer a detailed program to reverse the educational crisis of Black youth but to submit some issues needing consideration. The proposed federal Department of Education provides hope that an end to years of educational floundering can occur and new options can be pursued. Hopefully many strongly held beliefs—involving sacrosanct curriculum, busing, and teacher roles—can be shelved as the goals of secondary education are rethought. Current education must be brought into greater harmony with twentieth-century social and market demands. It must recognize the special differences of today's inner-city urban youth (who seek earlier marriages, independent functioning, and incomes and who hence need earlier job market entry) and the special obstructions (structural, racial, market constrictions, skills deficits, and vocational underexposure) that impede their chances to secure a living. Educational alternatives —such as school without walls, various work-education combinations, school apprenticeship, earlier technological training, and a broad range of differentiated educational routes to achievement—must be explored. Secondary education must provide clearer paths to occupational and functional roles in society if underclass entrapment is to be broken.

Black Community Networks

The last, and maybe the most difficult issue, is how to get Blacks themselves to help improve the Black context of living. To reverse the condition of underclass decay and suffering in the inner cities, greater attention must be given to the development of a permanent network of organizations, owned and operated by Blacks, which serve with greater efficacy the needs of the citizens of the community. No task is more formidable, challenging, and requiring of understanding than the one to institute a program of community-institutional development— the creation of an inner-city infrastructure.

The greatest weakness of the Black community today is the absence of a solid network of intermeshed organizations that provides a viable institutional base for the community. This factor alone contributes to a condition where the community remains underdeveloped, economically poor (as the flow of monies passes right through the community with very little being maintained by indigenous institutions for reinvestment), and dependent for services on agencies and businesses in which the poor have very little influence or determination. In the end, it is difficult for community members to do anything about large-scale poverty and unemployment when they do not control any large, indigenous economic organizations.

This picture, however, was not always as bleak, particularly in the human services area. For example, from the post-Civil War era through the early forties, indigenous local-based organizations formed the backbone of Black survival and progress. Human services agencies and educational, religious, and business organizations were created to respond to special needs of Blacks during those years. One can cite such organizations as the first benevolent mutual aid society, the Free African Society, which was founded in Philadelphia in 1787 and which had its origins in the Black Church. This organization provided support for the sick and benefits for widows and orphans. Organizations of this type proliferated at a great speed after the Civil War, and by 1830 over 100 such societies existed in Philadelphia alone. The Knights of Liberty and the Temple and Tabernacle of the Knights and Daughters of Tabor, a society claiming as many as 200,000 members by the turn of the century, offered a program "to help to spread religion, education, encourage land acquisition and temperance." Many mutual benefit societies also developed to respond to the need of Blacks for proper burial, and, ultimately, they served as economic enterprises providing insurance benefits for Blacks. Orphanages, institutions for the aged, nurseries and preschool classes, and homes for working girls (such as the Phillis Wheatley Home in Chicago or the Harriet Tubman homes in Boston) represent but a limited number of the institutions that serviced the Black community. However, in the past two and a half decades, that broad range of services has slowly fallen into disuse, and some enterprises have been allowed to die.

Various factors, some of which are evident from the foregoing discussion, have contributed to the decline of Black services: the continuous siphoning off of indigenous leaders from community-based activity into mainstream activity; the tendency of Blacks during the past few decades to increasingly rely on integrated and mainstream organizations to address Black concerns; the greater recognition and material reward accorded in mainstream success in contrast to that gained in the Black community; and, most significantly, the absence of a sound, indigenous economic base to maintain local institutions. Of course, it is understandable for Blacks to seek gains, opportunities, and, wherever possible, inroads within the mainstream. However, since the bulk of the Black community remains poor, continues to be underserved or inadequately served, and disproportionately carries the social burdens of poverty, unemployment, and joblessness, increased attention must be given to activities that strengthen the functional capacity of the Black community—simultaneous with efforts for progress in mainstream. The continuous outward flow of trained, skilled, and professional Blacks constitutes a real danger, as still-pervasive racism prevents inner-city residents from being able to rely on the mainstream institutional networks to provide quality services fairly. The need to maintain an indigenous organizational base to assure adequate and appropriate services to the people of the community is just as strong today as it was in the previous decades, since mainstream institutions continue to underserve Black interests or to serve them inappropriately.

To a large extent, the task facing Blacks in the eighties remains the same as that which the rebels of the sixties tried to address. Although their primary motive for developing independent, community-based enterprises was to secure incomes, finding alternatives to mainstream rejection was also an important goal. They sought legitimate means to meet sensitively the needs of inexperienced and underskilled workers and to simultaneously earn money within the Black community. Their small business attempts were intended to substitute for, not compete with, similar businesses in the mainstream. Unfortunately, as noted earlier, most of the initial ventures failed shortly after their creation—mainly because the initiators lacked managerial experience, there was no significant capital base to sustain the start-up period, and therefore the enterprises had too little time to become known, trusted, and used by the community. The few successes were usually supported by mainstream organizations, such as the Gas Station enterprise, which received help from Standard Oil of the private sector. Adequate support provided a period in which to gain experience and avert early bankruptcy. Other notable successes were in the human services areas, in the Youth Center program in Willowbrook and the Release-on-Own-Recognizance program run by members of the Sons of Watts—these supported by the public support. These initial attempts to build businesses and respond to a community need, though certainly modest, showed early recognition of the necessity of remedying the economic underdevelopment and lessening mainstream dependency of the ghetto.

The challenge to develop an institutional base in the Black community remains. In an economy where small businesses increasingly struggle to survive in competition with major oligopolies and corporate organizations, the challenge of building small Black enterprises does not appear to be an enviable one. Yet, some Black-owned income and service structures must operate if the lack of services, of employment, and of community influence among inner-city dwellers is to be corrected. The hesitancy with which this task has been faced reflects the need to answer some hard policy questions as well as some practical ones.

The main policy question, often involving ideological commitment, is whether Blacks should concentrate on combating institutional racism and gaining mainstream positions or whether they should focus on revitalizing the areas of Black living. And when the issue of institutional development is raised, the question becomes whether such an endeavor has any advantages for the future functioning of Blacks in the matters of the nation as a whole. Put in more common, although not necessarily more accurate terms, should movement toward integration or independent development be stressed? It may be recalled that in the sixties, community development, self-reliance, and local control were the cornerstones of such ghetto-based movements as the Black Panthers, the Sons of Watts, and Green Power, whereas the middle-income Blacks and new achievers stressed gaining and shoring up positions in the mainstream, especially those acquired as a result of the rebellions. These arguments have for too long dominated the decision making of Black activists and social analysts. The tendency has been to favor one or the other direction, as if they led to different objectives. But they do not. Those who have stressed reparative strategies have been attempting to develop a more functional environment, to promote Black survival by creating locally controlled economic opportunities. Those who have emphasized tactics to secure gains within the broader society have had a no less fervent commitment to better the condition of Blacks as a group. Both thrusts, therefore, have been and continue to be useful in advancing toward justice and economic equality. As long as this remains the goal, a wide range of activity is possible and necessary in different spheres at the same time.

Yet a balance must be maintained between the two prongs of such an overall strategy, and unfortunately in the past this balance has not been achieved. Especially during the late sixties and early seventies, most energy was expended on correcting the institutional inequities of white society and on getting Blacks into mainstream positions once racist restrictions had been eliminated. As a result, efforts to increase Black control over ghetto-reconstruction programs and services and to create Black-run institutions and businesses were neglected.

A strategy of community development is intended to provide not only greater economic solvency and better quality services but also institutional leverage on mainstream's organizational network so that the social causes of Blacks can be articulated and transmitted more effectively. An organizational base—an infrastructure—will ultimately allow inner-city people to meet their social needs with more self-reliance. Regrettably, some still see this thrust as divisive, even as contradictory to the main goal of Blacks. Hence the inner cities have suffered from a severe and continuous lack of attention, and even the few successful restoration programs, such as that in Bedford-Stuyvesant in Brooklyn, have often been considered secondary to mainstream endeavors. The fact is, however, that political activity aimed at improving the immediate condition of ghetto-encapsulated Blacks and increasing their capacity for independent functioning, both as individuals and as a community, boosts the vitality of all Blacks. Critics of this approach fail to see, or in some cases cannot accept, that most Americans are not really interested in correcting the ills of the ghetto. It is therefore up to Black themselves to become a strong force for social change of this environment. A crucial lesson to be learned about ethnic and minority survival in America is that no group has effectively moved from second-class or minority status to a self-determined place in American society without having in its control some economic and social service organizations supplying an institutional base.

The more practical and operational-oriented questions often raised by those considering local-based investment or institutional building are no less difficult to answer. For example, although very few question whether there is a service need in the community, many ask where the financial support to initiate such businesses will come from. Others express concern about the community's manpower capability, that is, the readily available labor base and professional expertise. Then there are those who cite the fact that very few small businesses based in the inner city are able to survive against the more formidable competitors who exist outside. And in the end, although not as frequently articulated, is the concern about the extreme hardship faced by those who choose to work daily within the inner-city enclaves of our devastated and depressed urban areas. Each question, in its own right, deserves elaborate attention, for each hits at the heart of issues that continue to make potential skilled and trained investors hesitant to undertake inner-city enterprises.

Suffice it to say that the question of capital support for business investment and development is crucial and not an easy one to deal with. There are resources that can be tapped— principally various federal and, in some cases, state programs that provide start-up funds for needed services, particularly in the inner cities. In the federal sector alone there are the Department of Housing and Urban Development (HUD), the Office of Child Development (OCD), the National Institute of Mental Health (NIMH), and various Health, Education, and Welfare (HEW) departments, to name a few. On the state level, departments of human social services, for example, provide resources to locally run programs. Some even provide minority business incentives. Unfortunately, as stated before, since there is no comprehensive rubric for securing (or for disbursing) these funds, a hodgepodge of different agency regulations, application forms, deadlines, monies disbursement procedures, and agency perspectives makes things extremely difficult for a small start-up company or entrepreneur. Ultimately this morass impinges on a local agency's ability to provide comprehensive services, and hence there is an increased fragmentation of service delivery systems. Often the burden created and the time demanded for administrative matters overshadows the energy and time available for service rendering and thus contributes to the venture's failure. Although funds are available, other methods must be considered, such as the Small Business Administration, local banks and loan associations, floating community shares, and other cooperative methods.

As to the question of manpower, one can with some pleasure express that this is one of the truly favorable areas in the equation. For qualified manpower and expertise now exist within the community in greater numbers than ever before. Only a cursory examination of the human services field discloses that, in almost every area of this industry, Blacks are performing vital roles, especially in terms of service rendering. The expertise is there, but here again, the true quality impact that this body could have on local-based services is not there. There is no question that there are supervisors, managers, practitioners, therapists, and community developers, but what is needed is investment in local service-based agencies.

Much more difficult is how to maintain a sound economic base for a program. It would be all well and good if equity existed and if the same principles that worked for small independent businesses in the past still worked today. But they do not. Therefore, some new factors must be brought into the economics of ghetto institutions. First, of course, must be the recognition that start-up businesses cannot be maintained on the meager economic base that has traditionally supported inner-city and ghetto businesses. Not only is there a need for a greater capital underpinning a business, but those who underwrite it must be prepared to provide a longer period of support. And those who undertake agency and services development must explore other models of economic organizations than those which have been traditionally tried by the individual entrepreneur. Various combinations—group investment, cooperatives, corporate or interagency interfacing, and community investment—that allow more than one investor to start up, run, and control a community service agency must be explored. In the end, perhaps even the bottom line, new small agency entrepreneurs must come to grips with the belief that one can gain both economic reward and personal gratification while providing community service; service cannot be a "get-rich-quick" scheme of getting rich off of the poverty and social displacement of others in the community.

Possibly, this last point is the crux of all that has been discussed in this chapter. The ills of the Black underclass are not going to be responded to, nor lasting cures sought, by anyone other than those whose interests are served by eradicating the social and economic conditions that produced this class. Irrespective of the threat that the underclass represents to the social balance of broader society, it poses an even more immediate problem of survival for the community of Blacks itself—the children, the parents, and the relatives of Black people. Some are obsolete and skilless, many are functional illiterates who cannot read or write; some are socially capable yet suffer from social want; many more are afraid of trying because the threat of disappointment, nonachievement, or rejection has become so great. Even as observers increasingly report that the Black thrust of the sixties is over, the problem grows more serious. It is no secret that having survived in the face of such oppressive conditions for so long, the hurt experienced by portions of the underclass finds expression in the continued occurrences of fratricide in the community. Black-on-Black crime increases, poor Blacks rip off not so poor Blacks, and only limited indigenous social control prevails. This condition, a direct reaction to want, exclusion, oppression, and need, cannot be ignored or go unattended. As long as the needs of the underclass of the community of Blacks are not addressed, there will continue to be separate and dysfunctional activity for survival. If the poor and middle-income, the job-seeking and working do not connect, a condition can be set in motion whereby those who are the most severely stricken and hurt by racism, deprivation, and poverty, and who are the most vunerable victims of institutional rejection, may out of desperation turn on and victimize their own community.

Community development speaks to the creation and development of institutions—political, economic, social, and human resources—that provide quality services to the local population. The broad range of human services needed—among them, vocational education, training, and placement; consumer and credit counseling for new wage earners; daycare and family guidance programs; cultural, recreational, and rehabilitation services for adolescents—can be partially provided by a local-based network that parallels some mainstream programs but that differs in its indigenous perspective and sensitivity. Developing local and community-neighborhood agencies does not mean separatism or withdrawal but rather that the achievers in the community assume greater responsibility for the nonachievers. At the same time, it means using a local institutional base to more effectively influence mainstream policies, program perspectives, and practices. Such a base could potentially counter and neutralize large-scale institutional rejection and social policies of benign neglect. But most of all it establishes the organizational superstructure for meeting the community's needs and for enhancing the people's thrust to shape their own destiny— at both the community and the national levels.

References

Birch, H. C., and Gussow, J. *Disadvantaged Children: Health, Nutrition, and School Failure*. New York: Harcourt, Brace, Jovanovich, 1970.

Clark, K. B. *Dark Ghetto: Dilemmas of Social Power*. New York: Harper & Row, 1965.

Cohen, N. (Ed.). *The Los Angeles Riots: A Socio-Psychological Study*. (Published in cooperation with the Institute of Government and Public Affairs, University of California, Los Angeles.) New York: Praeger, 1970.

Coleman, J. S. *Equality of Educational Opportunity*. Washington, D.C.: U.S. Office of Education, 1966.

Conot, R. *Rivers of Blood, Years of Darkness*. New York: Bantam Books, 1976.

Cordesco, F. "Teaching the Puerto Rican Experience." In J. S. Banks (Ed.), *Teaching Ethnic Studies: Concepts and Strategies*. Washington, D.C.: National Council for the Social Studies, 1973.

Cruse, H. *The Crisis of the Negro Intellectual, From Its Origins to the Present*. New York: Morrow, 1967.

Derbyshire, R., and Brody, E. B. "Marginality, Identity, and Behavior in the American Negro: A Functional Analysis." *International Journal of Social Psychiatry*, 1964, *10* (1), 7–13.

Dervin, B., and Greenberg, B. S. *The Communication Environment of the Urban Poor*. (Report no. 15 of a six-year project.) East Lansing: Michigan State University, 1972.

Dickeman, M. "Teaching Cultural Pluralism." In J. A. Banks (Ed.), *Teaching Ethnic Studies: Concepts and Strategies*. Washington, D.C.: National Council for the Social Studies, 1973.

Dollard, J. *Caste and Class in a Southern Town*. (3rd ed.) New York: Doubleday, 1949.

Donovan, J. C. *The Politics of Poverty*. New York: Pegasus, 1967.

Drake, S., and Cayton, H. R. *Black Metropolis: A Study of Negro Life in a Northern City*. Vol. 1. (Rev. ed.) New York: Harcourt Brace Jovanovich, 1970.

Dunbar, E., and others. "A Delinquency Prevention Program for Watts." Unpublished research protocol for Program of Special Services for Groups, Inc., Los Angeles, 1967.

Edelman, M. W. "The Black Family in the Changing Cities." In *Better Cities for a Better Nation*, Proceedings of the 68th National Urban League Conference, Los Angeles, August 6–9, 1978. New York: National Urban League, 1979.

Erikson, E. H. "The Concept of Identity in Race Relations: Notes and Queries." *Daedalus*, 1966, *95*, 145–214.

Fantini, M., and Weinstein, G. *The Disadvantaged: Challenge to Education*. New York: Harper & Row, 1968.

Fisher, L. H. *The Problem of Violence: Observations on Race Conflict in Los Angeles*. New York: American Council on Race Relations, 1947.

Frazier, F. E. *Black Bourgeoisie: The Rise of the New Middle Class*. New York: Free Press, 1956.

Friedman, M. *Capitalism and Freedom*. Chicago: University of Chicago Press, 1962.

Glazer, N., and Moynihan, D. P. *Beyond the Melting Pot*. Cambridge, Mass.: M.I.T. Press, 1967.

Gordon, E. W. "Decentralization and Educational Reform." *IRCD Bulletin*, 1968, *4* (5); and 1969, *5* (1), 1–5.

Grier, W. H., and Cobbs, P. M. *Black Rage*. New York: Bantam

Books, 1968.

Hare, N. *The Black Anglo-Saxons*. New York: Marzani and Munsell, 1965.

Harrington, M. *The Other America: Poverty in the United States.* Baltimore: Penguin Books, 1966.

Hill, R. B. *The Strengths of Black Families*. New York: National Urban League, 1972.

Hodge, R. W., Siegel, P. M., and Rossi, P. H. "Occupational Prestige in the U.S.: 1925–1963." In R. Bendix and S. M. Lipset, *Class, Status, and Power: Social Stratification in Comparative Perspective*. (2nd ed.) New York: Free Press, 1966.

Horner, V. "Misconceptions Concerning Language in the Disadvantaged." *IRCD Bulletin*, 1966, *2* (3a), 1–2.

Kardiner, A., and Ovesey, L. *The Mark of Oppression: Explorations in the Personality of the American Negro*. Cleveland, Ohio: Collins, William, and World Publishing, 1964.

Karon, B. P. *The Negro Personality: A Rigorous Investigation of the Effects of Culture*. New York: Springer, 1964.

Kerner, O. (Chrm.). *Report of the National Advisory Commission on Civil Disorders*. Washington, D.C.: U.S. Government Printing Office, 1968.

Kimbrough, R. B. *Political Power and Educational Decision Making*. Chicago: Rand McNally, 1964.

Leichter, H. J. "The Concept of Educative Style." *Teachers College Record*, 1973, *75*, 239–250.

McAdoo, H. P. "Black Kinship." *Psychology Today*, 1979, *12* (12), 67–110.

McCone, J. A. *Violence in the City—An End or a Beginning?* Report by the Governor's Commission on the Los Angeles Riots. Columbia, Miss.: Lucas, 1965.

McCord, W., and others. *Life-Styles in the Black Ghetto*. New York: Norton, 1969.

Meeker, M. *Background for Planning*. Research Report No. 17. Los Angeles: Research Department, Welfare Planning Council, 1964.

Meissner, H. H. (Ed.). *Poverty in the Affluent Society*. New

York: Harper & Row, 1966.

Osofsky, G. *Harlem: The Making of a Ghetto*. New York: Harper & Row, 1966.

Pettigrew, T. F. *Profile of the American Negro*. New York: D. Van Nostrand, 1964.

Rainwater, L., and Yancey, W. L. *The Moynihan Report and the Politics of Controversy*. Cambridge, Mass.: M.I.T. Press, 1967.

Raskin, M. "Political Socialization in the Schools." *Harvard Educational Review*, 1968, *38* (3), 550–553.

Riis, J. *Jacob Riis Revisited: Poverty in the Slum of Another Era*. New York: Doubleday, 1968.

Robinson, D. *Chance to Belong: Story of the Los Angeles Youth Project, 1943–1949*. New York: Woman's Press, 1949.

Scanzoni, J. H. *The Black Family in Modern Society*. Boston: Allyn & Bacon, 1971.

Sherman, R. B. *The Negro and the City*. Englewood Cliffs, N.J.: Prentice-Hall, 1970.

Taba, H., and Elkins, D. *Teaching Strategies for the Culturally Disadvantaged*. Chicago: Rand McNally, 1966.

Tidwell, B. J. "The Sons of Watts Improvement Association's Self-Training Programs." Unpublished report, Los Angeles, 1966.

U.S. Bureau of the Census. *The Social and Economic Status of the Black Population in the United States: An Historical View, 1790–1978*. Current Population Reports, Special Studies Series P–23, No. 80. Washington, D.C.: U.S. Government Printing Office, 1979.

U.S. Commission on Civil Rights. *Racial Isolation in the Public Schools*. Washington, D.C.: U.S. Government Printing Office, 1976.

Valentine, C. A. *Culture and Poverty: Critique and Counterproposals*. Chicago: University of Chicago Press, 1968.

Will, R. E., and Vatter, H. G. (Eds). *Poverty in Affluence: The Social, Political, and Economic Dimension of Poverty in the United States*. (2nd ed.) New York: Harcourt Brace Jovanovich, 1970.

Williams, J. D. (Ed.). *The State of Black America 1979*. New York: National Urban League, 1979.

Wilson, D., and Lantz, E. "The Effect of Cultural Change on the Negro Race in Virginia, As Indicated by a Study of State Hospital Admissions." *American Journal of Psychiatry*, 1957, *114*, 25–32.

Wilson, W. J. *The Declining Significance of Race: Blacks and Changing American Institutions*. Chicago: University of Chicago Press, 1978.

Wolf, R. "The Measurement of Environments." In *Proceedings of the 1964 Invitational Conference on Testing Problems*. Princeton, N.J.: Educational Testing Service, 1965.

Zigler, E. "Mental Retardation: Current Issues and Approaches." In L. W. Hoffman and M. Hoffman (Eds.), *Review of Child Development Research*. New York: Russell Sage Foundation, 1966.

Index